*H*ANOTHÉR *Hannah*

Liz...

God's blessing
on you♥

Mary Klassen

Mari Klassen

ANOTHER HANNAH

All scripture quotations, unless otherwise indicated, are taken from the Holy Bible, New International Version®, NIV®. Copyright ©1973, 1978, 1984 by Biblica, Inc.™ Used by permission of Zondervan. All rights reserved worldwide. Scripture quotations marked (NLT) are taken from the Holy Bible, New Living Translation, copyright © 1996, 2004, 2007 by Tyndale House Foundation. Used by permission of Tyndale House Publishers, Inc., Carol Stream, Illinois 60188. All rights reserved. Scripture quotations marked (KJV) are taken from the Holy Bible, King James Version, which is in the public domain. Scripture quotations marked (ESV) are taken from The Holy Bible, English Standard Version® (ESV®), copyright © 2001 by Crossway, a publishing ministry of Good News Publishers. Used by permission. All rights reserved.

Author photo courtesy of Jodi Klassen, of Photography by Jodi. (www.photosbyjodi.com)

ISBN: 978-1-77069-268-8

Printed in Canada

Word Alive Press
131 Cordite Road, Winnipeg, MB R3W 1S1
www.wordalivepress.ca

Library and Archives Canada Cataloguing in Publication

Klassen, Mari, 1945
    Another Hannah / Mari Klassen.

ISBN 978-1-77069-268-8

    1. Klassen, Mari, 1945-. 2. Mennonites--Saskatchewan--Biography. 3. Mennonites--Manitoba--Biography. 4. God (Christianity)--Faithfulness. I. Title.

BX8143.K63A3 2011   289.7092   C2011-901686-9

Dedication

I want to dedicate this book to our children—Melissa, Samuella, Maria, Nathaniel, and David. After all, it is about you and how God gave you to us. These are the blessings we prayed over you as you became adults:

Melissa Shelene. The name Melissa means "honeybee," with the connotation of having pleasant companionship with one's friends or associates. Your middle name, Shelene, means "gentle lamb." And this is exactly who you are.

Your sweet, gentle nature is a blessing to us and everyone you come into contact with. We speak God's blessing of gentleness into your life. May the Holy Spirit guide you in your giving and may your heart receive the gifts He has for you. God bless your generous and caring heart.

Your name was in my heart before you ever came into our lives. I didn't know why I wanted to call you Melissa, but when your Auntie Helen heard your name, she said to me, "I know why you named her

Melissa. When you were a little girl, Mom used to call you Meena Kjleena Meleeza, meaning 'my little Melissa.' She used it as a term of endearment." So, you see, Melissa, I gave you *my* name... the one that affirmed me as a wanted, precious child. You are my wanted, precious child. We prayed that God would choose a child for us, and we never doubted that you were His choice. I am privileged and blessed to be chosen to be your mother.

We speak blessings on you as you serve the Lord with your gift of music in piano teaching and praise and worship. May God bless you also in your role as wife and mother. May your children rise up and call you blessed. May the blessing of the Lord be upon you and cause you to prosper in whatever you set your hands to do.

Zephaniah 3:17 says, *"The Lord your God is with you, he is mighty to save. He will take great delight in you, he will quiet you with his love, he will rejoice over you with singing."*

As you sing out your love to Him in that beautiful voice of yours, remember that He also is singing back to you, delighting in who you are... His child.

Samuella. You were the one we prayed so long for, the fulfillment of God's promise of natural children. And yet we had promised to give you back to God just like Hannah in the Bible did, as He so gently reminded me. However, He blessed me greatly with His presence in the process of your release back to Him.

The following poem was written when one of your little cousins also left for heaven before experiencing earth, and it is true of our feelings for you as well:

My precious little baby...
You spent so little time inside of me...
You took up so little space in my womb...
Yet you filled my whole heart
With so much love and hope.
I know I must release you, my precious baby...
To Someone whose heart is much bigger than mine,
Whose ways are much higher than mine.

Father, as I give you my baby,
Hold her close, hold me and her daddy close...
And may we touch one another in that embrace...
And may our healing begin there...
Amen.

I look forward to meeting you in Heaven, my little Samuella, now a grown woman in the presence of God.

Maria Rochelle. The name Maria means "living fragrance." The name contains a spiritual connection to 2 Corinthians 2:14: *"But thanks be to God, who always leads us in triumphal procession in Christ and through us spreads everywhere the fragrance of the knowledge of him. For we are to God the aroma of Christ among those who are being saved and those who are perishing."*

Your second name, Rochelle, means "little rock." You are the small rock fashioned after the chief cornerstone, the Rock Christ Jesus. You are strong in the Lord, the fragrance of Christ, showing consideration of others by your gentle and humble spirit. People catch a whiff of Jesus when you come into a room. You are of the highest quality, a miracle sent by God to delight and fulfill the deep longings of my heart... a lasting fragrance. I speak the full blessing of your name into your life, having given you my name, which was also my mother's name.

Right from birth, you have been a delight with your inquisitive nature and bubbly personality. From an early age, you have set your heart on the pursuit of knowledge, and your every effort has been rewarded with excellence, as can be seen in your teaching. God's anointing is also on your musical gifting as you lead praise and worship. May God continue to guide and keep you as you walk in the destiny and purposes He has for your life. He will be both your rear-guard and front-guard, and whatever you set your hand to do will be successful.

You are a sweet fragrance, a woman after God's own heart. He is using you in mighty ways. Just as we waited for you to come in God's time and in His way, may all His promises to you be fulfilled in His time and in His way.

Nathaniel Reuben. The name Nathaniel means "God has given," and your middle name, Reuben, means "Behold, a son." Therefore you are the son that God has given in answer to our prayers: "And please, Lord, let it be a son this time."

Just as Jesus' disciple Nathaniel, we believe your destiny is to live a life "without guile." We believe Jesus is also saying to you that you will see greater things happening in your life than you will ever ask or think.

May you be released to follow God's path for your life, seeking to please your heavenly Father as you have been pleasing us. We love you, Nathan, and are proud of you. You have the ability to relate to people and speak into their lives, as we see you do in your teaching. You have a keen desire for knowledge and an eagerness to pursue truth... you are ever-growing in wisdom. Jesus says, *"Blessed are the meek, for they will inherit the earth"* (Matthew 5:5). Through meekness and integrity, God will use you to touch your generation for Him.

May the Godly heritage of your grandparents continue to the fourth and fifth generations. *"You will be blessed when you come in and blessed when you go out"* (Deuteronomy 28:6). May God bless you in your marriage to Stephanie, a Godly woman, handpicked by the One who delights in you, Nathan... as do we.

David Patrick. Obviously, you are named after the David in the Bible. David means "beloved, dearly beloved." My scripture for you is Deuteronomy 33:12, which says, *"Let the beloved of the Lord rest secure in him, for he shields him all day long."* Patrick means "noble one." As a child of God, you have a noble calling to *"declare the praises of him who called you out of darkness into his wonderful light"* (1 Peter 2:9).

The Biblical David was anointed to fulfill an important role in the kingdom of Israel. So also, you have been blessed with a kingly anointing for your work in the kingdom of God. Therefore, go in His strength, courage, and the mighty name of God. You are a defender of the faith... a modern giant slayer.

I pray a blessing over your keen mind and your zest for life and work. May God protect you from all evil and abundantly bless the work of your hands. You are a great friend to many; always blessing them with wit and humour. You are gifted in giving praise to God through music, and it is a sweet sound in His ear—yes, even the booming sound of your drums!

I speak into your life a blessing of humble trust in God. May you prosper in health, wealth, and peace as together with your sweet wife you seek to honour God as you do life. I am blessed to be your mother and excited to watch how God is developing you into a man after His own heart.

Table of Contents

Foreword

Mari was my close friend as we journeyed together spiritually. One of the happenings on our journey together was attending a conference on the Holy Spirit in Brandon. I was in the prayer room with Mari and Ruben when the curly-haired lady asked for prayer for a safe pregnancy and Mari burst into tears.

After a while, Ruben shared their burden of not being able to have children naturally. Everyone in the room gathered around them and prayed for them. We all had such a spirit of rejoicing that we left there confident that God was answering this prayer.

Through the years I have always felt part of the family. Their children, even though they're all grown up, still call me Auntie Grace. I feel privileged to have witnessed the miracles of these children.

– Grace Murray

Introduction

Two-year-old Mari wandered around the big farm kitchen, asking for a drink of water. Everyone was too busy to pay any attention; the guys were working on a repair job of some kind, the rest were busy keeping out of their way.

Finally little Mari spotted a cup on the windowsill and reached for it. No one stopped her until she started coughing in great distress. What she thought was water was actually kerosene, put there by her brothers who were working on their project. Mother came running, picked up the now limp little girl, and took her outside where she pummelled her on the back, hoping desperately to bring life back to the seemingly lifeless child.

The family looked on in sad silence. A pervasive sense of hopelessness settled amongst them, and yet Mother would not stop. She couldn't, for in her inner being she sensed the urging of One who was higher than this moment: "Keep going; she must not die; I have a special purpose for her life." After a few more heart-wrenching moments of coaxing life back, the child finally drew breath again and a collective sigh of relief and gratitude went up.

Mari lived, and here is her story—a story of God's purpose for her life fulfilled, a life of the unexpected, of miracles never imagined, a story that begs to be told so others will be encouraged to believe in the God of the impossible.

CHAPTER ONE

Humble Beginnings

I was born at home on a farm near Hague, Saskatchewan, the seventh in a family of nine children. The second one had died at six months; pneumonia was not as curable as it is today. He was the second son. After that there was a daughter followed by three more sons. The daughter was Helena (Helen, for short) and she was getting impatient for a sister.

When I finally arrived, Helen was given the privilege of naming me. She named me Maria, after our mother, Maria Loeppky, the daughter of Johann Loeppky, bishop of the Old Colony Mennonite Conference since 1930. Our father was Abraham R. Derksen. He and mother started out on a small farm near Hague that he had inherited from our Grandfather Derksen. However, Dad still had to secure a loan to cover the expenses of starting a farm, one of which was building our house.

Things seemed okay in the beginning, but then the Great Depression hit that area of Saskatchewan very hard and it affected us, as well as most of the people around us. Our farm was not doing well and Mother was not doing well, either. She needed to get away from the isolation of our farm. She wanted to move to a village setting, preferably one with a church, where she could have fellowship with other people. Plans were made to move to the small village of Reinland, near Osler.

My Loeppky grandparents lived in Reinland, but they were soon going to be moving to Mexico to help with the Mennonite work there. Grandfather Loeppky had been one of the original ministers traveling to Mexico to scout out a suitable area for the first Mennonite migration. Although the Mennonites enjoyed religious freedom and a prosperous farming situation in Canada, there was a problem with their German schools. The Manitoba and Saskatchewan governments were no longer allowing anything but English schools. This was a serious situation for the Mennonites. They valued the German language as a means of preserving their faith and culture. Therefore, a huge group of Mennonites moved to Mexico in the early 1900s. In 1948, Grandfather felt he was needed there. Their house in Reinland was where our mother had grown up and since it was now available, it would become our new home.

I was almost three years old at the time and remember moving to this house. It was dark when we arrived in our horse-drawn Bennet wagon. I was so tired, but I tried to keep up with Mother as Grandmother explained which rooms were assigned to us. I kept wondering (probably out loud in a whining voice), "Where is my bed?"

About a year later, our grandparents returned from Mexico. Bishop Loeppky, apparently, was much too liberal for the extremely conservative ministerial that moved against him in Mexico, so they moved back to the village of Neuhorst, Saskatchewan, where he resumed his role as Bishop of the Old Colony Mennonite churches of Canada.

After we'd lived in Reinland for a while, we lost our farm. This was a very difficult time in our father's life. He had suffered a blow to his head as a young boy when he was sent out to close the barn door during a storm. The door banged him on the head and he fell unconscious. This injury created a mass on his brain which seemed to lie dormant until later in his adult years. Whenever he experienced times of great stress, he would be greatly affected. It was definitely affecting him at this time, and even though our financial state was improved, we now had a father who seemed to be living in his own world, unable to cope with reality. Mother had to compensate and be the strong one in the family. This was quite stressful for her.

However, Dad seemed to come alive at Christmas time, almost as if he were living a fantasy. Even though we were still very poor, he made sure it was a very happy time for us as he and Mom shopped for our gifts. On Christmas Eve, we would eagerly put out our respective bowls. The size of the bowls reflected seniority... the oldest had the biggest bowl! We could hardly sleep at night for excitement.

When Dad finally said it was a reasonable hour, he would get up and make a fire. Our house had little insulation and was very cold in the mornings. Then we would all line up from oldest to youngest at the door to the big kitchen/dining room. Finally it was opened and we rushed to the table, which had been covered with a large sheet.

Gift-wrapping was not done, in keeping with the simplicity taught in our faith. When the sheet came off, we saw everything at once and just let out a scream of delight! Dad (Santa Claus) was enjoying it all just as much as we were.

We were never ashamed to tell our friends what we got for Christmas; our gifts sometimes surpassed those whose parents were wealthy. We got nice dolls, toy trucks, and things we had asked for, but always included in our bowls were drawing and colouring books with pencils and new crayons. We would have been disappointed if these were not there, because we were all quite artistic and spent a lot of time drawing. At school, all the Derksens got A's in art class. Often in the summer, when there were thunderstorms, we would get out our drawing and colouring books and have our own art class. Drawing had a calming effect and we would hardly notice the storm.

From the age of two until the age of sixteen, I lived in this very sheltered Mennonite setting. Most of the villagers were as poor as we were, having also suffered a setback during the Depression. We lived in a large house with a summer kitchen connecting it to the barn. My father modified this summer kitchen, especially working on the chimney. What a relief it was to move into it when summer came. We would move our table, some cupboards, and sometimes even the stove—along with dishes and the cream separator!

The summer kitchen was quite a large area and we did most of our "living" here. Doing the canning, cooking, and baking here kept the rest of the house cool. Even our Sunday visiting was done in the summer kitchen on occasion. When company came, we would often indulge in cracking sunflower seeds. These were roasted in a pan in the oven and were so good! Spitting your sunflower seed shells on the floor was normally frowned upon, but the summer kitchen had a cement floor, so we got away with it. We would sweep them up by sprinkling sawdust on the floor first… it seemed to make the job easier!

The rest of the house was kept cool by drawing all the blinds and closing doors behind us if we absolutely needed to go into that part of the house. Of course, our bedrooms were there and we kept them cool by opening windows in the evenings and letting in the breeze.

We had no land to work, so our livestock was important to us. We only had a few cows, pigs, and chickens, but they supplied us with milk, eggs, and meat. Each fall there would be a pig butchering event, with neighbours helping for a whole day. It was an exciting day; we'd get up very early to prepare. There would always be a delicious meal of roasted chicken at noon. My job was usually scraping the intestines for use in sausage-making. After this day we had ham, farmer sausage, and various other cuts of pork that would last us for the whole year.

I had two dogs that I absolutely adored, but because they were not contributing anything to the workload they were considered an added expense. One of the dogs came from a farm two miles away. When the time came to pick him up, my little sister and I took a sack and our little red wagon. It seemed we had walked forever before we reached the farm. We had no idea it was so far away! We also had never been to this place before and were not even sure we were going the right way. At last we arrived, and after giving them one dollar I got to take my little black puppy home. He was so small that he could walk under our other dog, a medium-sized terrier. Later he grew very large and the terrier could walk under him!

My mother used to tease me for being so motherly with my dogs. At night they had to be home, so I would call and call them. She said they were just making a game of it. When they didn't come, I'd go back to Mother and announce that I would give them a huge spanking when they got home. When they finally came running home at top speed, I greeted them with open arms... something like the greeting of the Prodigal Son. For some reason, I just couldn't spank them, which was probably why this "game" repeated itself night after night. No wonder Mother just chuckled at my idle threats!

Sadly, both dogs had to be put down one winter, because night after night they would pester the helpless cows in the barn, sometimes even biting their tails. Mother knew how hard this was for me, so she made sure I was told about this in advance. She promised me two new pairs of socks, which I could go and pick out myself at the store. I came home with a heavy heart after school that day, knowing my delightful Teddy and Scotty would never again be there to greet me. The socks were a very inadequate substitute, to say the least!

We had a big garden and a large cherry orchard that certainly kept us busy all summer. My five brothers all enjoyed making things. In the summer, my younger siblings—Anna and Ike—and I would each get a handmade "vehicle" of their creation. We "paid" for them by hoeing extra rows in the garden. (Were we hoeing their rows? I never knew for sure.) However, we really enjoyed the little two-wheeled carts they made for us. We scooted around with them among the cherry trees.

During this carefree preteen life, I remember an incident that scared my mother and caused me to realize the value of life. Our neighbours had a beautiful horse. It had been a show horse at one time, but now it was old and had been put out to pasture. The problem was that the horse occasionally considered our yard his pasture. I would take a carrot and lure him back to the neighbours' land, carefully closing the gate behind me. My mother once watched me do this from the front porch where she would often sit and rest in the evenings. I had managed to get him to his side of the gate, had given him his carrot, and then turned around to go back. As I closed the gate and returned to the porch I looked up to see that my mother had turned pale. She told me the horse had reared as I turned to go and his hooves had just missed me as I had slipped away through the gate!

Perhaps once again she sensed that I was meant to live, for a purpose God had yet to bring about. At any rate, the incident sobered me as well.

I was now twelve years old and had no recollection of our destitute life before Reinland. We were still poor, but so was everyone else in this little village. Because we were on welfare, however, we had enough food and clothes, a school close enough to walk to, and friends. What more could a young girl want? But I did want more.

I was dissatisfied with the religion around me; I felt stifled. I seemed to be breaking all the rules, especially when it came to clothes. My older sister sewed our dresses and she was very creative. We would order the material from the Eaton's catalogue, then Helen would take it home with her. When she brought the finished creation back, we were always so excited. There were always ruffles, bows, and other stylish ways of setting us off from the others. They definitely went beyond the ultra-conservative norm of no frills, so I was labeled *shtolt*, meaning prideful or frivolous.

The basic elements in our faith were humility and simplicity. These elements were expressed in the wearing of plain clothes and having no modern conveniences, such as electricity or telephone (even though the poles came right through our big garden). We could have nothing that would encourage materialism in any way. When my grandfather died, the next bishop bought a car, which raised a few eyebrows since cars represented the modern trend of the day. But because the car was black, it was acceptable.

Black was a predominating colour in dress as well. My older sister got married in the customary black dress. However, after the usual reception, there was a party where the clergy was not in attendance. Here she wore a pretty blue party dress that her fiancé, Dick Wiebe, had bought for her. There was even lively music and dancing. After a while, others had parties at their weddings as well and it became acceptable, although not openly condoned.

To their credit, parents and clergy had only the spiritual protection of their young people at heart. But that wasn't how I saw it at that age. I wanted pretty things; I wanted shorter hair with curls instead of the braids and ponytails we all wore. I was considered a bit of a rebel.

But my heart was spiritually hungry... I wasn't sure where I stood with God. Was He just someone who was there waiting to punish me for breaking the rules? There had to be something more.

It was during this time of spiritual searching that my older brothers went to work in the big city. They came back not all worldly and corrupted like Mother had feared, but something much worse! They had changed religions! Every weekend they would come home, bubbling over with the joy of their newfound salvation, which caused great distress for our mother.

They had already pushed our parents' limits with all their music. Instruments were not allowed, but our oldest brother John had acquired a guitar for himself and a fiddle for Bill. Abe found a banjo that he really liked and paid for it with his own hard-earned money. They formed a band that played at amateur hours and house gatherings. There were always a lot of young people coming to our house to listen to their music and we younger children took it all for granted after a while. The singer they emulated was always Hank Snow, and we younger ones had better not mention any other singer as our favourite!

Bill and Abe even played in a band that had a half-hour segment on the radio every Saturday night. They naively called themselves "The Country Playboys" (meaning boys from the country who liked to play instruments)! We eagerly listened to them on our battery-operated radio, hoping the battery would last until the end of the program.

Fifty years later, the brothers are still playing together occasionally and they actually recorded a CD in 2005, doing their old numbers. They held a concert in Osler at that time as well, which was completely packed out. In fact, many had to be turned away because there just wasn't enough room. Most of those in attendance were of Old Colony Mennonite background, which was a balm to our formerly rejected hearts. They did another concert at Providence College in Manitoba, which was also a huge success. John even got to go to Nova Scotia a few years ago, doing a half-hour segment of Hank Snow songs at the Hank Snow Music Tribute Centre. In fact, Hank Snow's backup band, The Rainbow Ranch Boys, was there as well, and played with him!

All this forbidden music, however, put our parents in a difficult position with the clergy. As if all this wasn't enough, they now had to deal with the fallout of this new "religious experience" that our brothers so eagerly talked about!

CHAPTER TWO

Hope-Filled Beginnings

We younger ones could see that something had happened to our brothers spiritually and we wanted what they had. They were even holding back on their "worldly" music because of finding the Lord. We eagerly looked forward to the weekends, hoping they would take us along to their church, the one with the lively music and friendly people. Here we experienced much freedom and love as the Gospel was shared. It rang so true in my heart and I wanted it so much. My brothers left us some tracts which explained how to receive Jesus into our hearts.

One day, I took the tract to my room and knelt by my bed, following the guidelines written on it. I knew that I could know for sure that I was a Christian and that heaven would be mine, because Jesus made it very clear in John 3:16—*"For God so loved the world that he gave his only Son, so that everyone who believes in him will not perish but have eternal life"* (NLT).

The word "have" in this verse was very reassuring; I just needed to believe that when Jesus died on the cross to pay the price for my sin, it was enough. I could not add to it with my actions or even with a humble, righteous life. I only needed to trust in what He had done, not in what I could do, to prove my worth. Neither could I hope that my attitude of humility would convince Him at the Judgment Seat that I was somehow eligible for heaven. However, as I would receive what He had done for me and put my trust only in His work for me, I would want to live a humble and righteous life in return. I would also want to share with others His marvellous grace, forgiveness and the assurance of this salvation.

When I got up from following these guidelines, I didn't feel much different, but I did have a determination in my heart to live my life according to this new truth. Even though I shared this tract with my friends and didn't hesitate to tell them about it, I myself didn't actually have full assurance of salvation until much later. Assurance of salvation was not preached in our conservative Old Colony church, because it sounded too presumptuous and didn't line up with the church's teachings of humility where salvation could only be hoped for. Perhaps that is why this was an issue for me even while I was sharing my newfound faith.

But share I did, and I even managed to convert my two best friends! I also made enemies and found out quickly at age twelve that those older than me also had greater power. My friend's older sister told her not to associate with me. We still did so, somewhat secretly at times.

We made mailboxes at the end of our driveways and had a system of letting each other know when there was a letter. We even had a Bible Club going where more of my friends came. Several of these friends, as well as my best friend's older sister, are following the Lord to this day. Praise God, He was able to use my faltering efforts.

I remember my feelings of loneliness mixed with newfound joy. Nobody around me understood this new truth. I was misunderstood, even in my own home. My brothers had come home full of joy and excitement, but it seemed they had also caused a disturbance in our home. They would argue with our mother to the point of heated discussions. Dad didn't get involved, but he was quietly supportive of Mom.

Even though I was on my brothers' "side," so to speak, I saw the price that was paid: turmoil, division, and confusion in our family. In time, as my mother processed all this, she came to a place of peace. She even came to my brother's baptism, which was held at this other church, and she was moved to tears. After the baptism, the heated discussions never resumed.

Mom had often shared with us her conversion experience, when she was a young girl. She had witnessed several fits of epilepsy in a young child, and this bothered her a lot. It bothered her so much, in fact, that she made a plea with God: "I'll give my life to you if only I won't have to see that again." Her prayer was answered and Mother continued to live a devoted, prayerful life for Him. Our parents' bedroom was in one corner of the very large living room. We tried not to enter it after Mother had retired for bed. If we did, we would often find her on her knees, praying for all of us.

My brothers' experience, especially in the setting of the "forbidden church," put her on guard, however. She was always carefully watched in the community since she was the daughter of the bishop, and she felt those judging eyes keenly. We found out later that even though she had been confronted with her sons' digressions, she strongly defended them. But even as dissension surrounded us in our community, there was peace in our home.

I begged to go along when my brothers went to their new church, and sometimes I was allowed to go. What a joy it was to sing these new songs, to fellowship with like-minded people who were so friendly and accepting of us! My heart yearned to be there all the time. But I also sensed my mother's dilemma and tried to honour her wishes. Often I would pray earnestly that God would open a way for me to be a part of an Evangelical church such as the one my brothers attended.

My other longing was to be able to go to high school, or at least take it by correspondence. This just didn't happen in our conservative Mennonite community. Young people never went beyond Grade Eight, because higher education might encourage "worldliness," or even leaving the faith. After finishing Grade Eight, or upon reaching their fifteenth birthday, they would quit school—the girls to prepare for their role as future homemakers and the boys to help on the farm.

Throughout Grade Eight, I pondered and prayed, trying not to mention to Mom my longing for high school; she was, after all, waiting for me to finally be at home to help her. My older sister was nine years older than me and had been married and away from home for some years now.

Finally, during the end of the school year, I worked up the courage to ask if I could go to high school. Imagine my surprise when she said yes! Apparently my older brothers had been advocating for me. Abe investigated and found out that there was going to be a school bus coming right past our place, taking students to the new high school in Osler. My brother Bill had already checked out the books I would need and was prepared to pay for them. All of this came as a complete surprise to me. Perhaps Mother was sensitive to the same Voice that urged her to keep pummelling me when I nearly died as a child, telling her now that I was meant to go on to higher education and would not stay in this village as the other girls did.

In any case, it seemed she was willing to sacrifice the help she had long been waiting for. She was also once again risking the criticism of the clergy, since higher education was frowned upon, to say the least. My brothers, aware of my dream of high school, were doing their best to make it come true! I was completely overwhelmed, and praised God that whole summer for His wonderful answer to prayer.

So in the fall of 1961, I, the shy fifteen-year-old girl from the village of Reinland, was off to high school. I was making history in our little village, but with "shunning" overtones. No one had ever gone to high school from my community and no one was applauding me! Most of my new friends were the kids I went to high school with. Two Christian girls approached me at my new school and included me in their duo... changing our status to trio (and we actually did sing as a trio after a while).

I felt like I was living in two completely different worlds. My one world was at home in my little village with the limited view I had always known. My other world was in high school where I had new, accepting friends, books and learning to my heart's content, and the opportunity to sing in the glee club. Oh, how I loved singing). Generally speaking, new vistas were ahead of me. ("New Vistas Ahead" was our class's graduation theme, but I experienced it most dramatically when I entered Grade Nine.)

It was a good school; the principal and some of the teachers were Christians. There was an Inter-School Christian Fellowship which I attended with my many Christian friends, and I just thrived in this new life. I applied myself to my studies with great diligence.

In my other world back in the village, my mother seemed to be working too hard and I was torn. Sometimes she would ask me to stay home and help her, but when she saw the great hesitation on my part she relented and let me go. This came back to bless her at the end of the ninth grade, when I came home in the middle of June with all my books. She was in the garden when I got off the bus and asked me why I had brought all my books home, to which I replied, "I quit school!" She was quite irate with me until I told her I was only joking. I actually had been exempted from writing all eight of the provincial exams! She was overjoyed, because now she would have my help sooner than she'd expected. The exemption criteria were high marks and perfect to near-perfect attendance.

With summer coming, I once again entered the world of conservative village life, but this time it was more peaceful. One incident that revealed the peace in our home came on a Sunday afternoon at *faspa* time (a light meal in the afternoon). My brother-in-law Dick and sister Helen were there as well. Dick had just said how he was so glad that his sins were forgiven and for the assurance of knowing he would go to heaven when he died. I braced myself for the inevitable—Mom would be upset, because this was a boastful statement that was akin to blasphemy in her faith. But she was calm and peaceful as she gently commented, "And I'm glad that I can say that, too." This was the single most blessed moment of my life to that point.

That summer, my mother and I worked well together, finally enjoying a peaceful relationship. Where before there had been an undercurrent of discord with me wanting to go to the "other" church and she wanting me to stay the course as she knew it, we now just enjoyed each other. I knew I needed to live out my newfound faith and not hound her with the things I wanted.

Even though I knew not to hound, there was one thing I really did want: to go and stay at my sister's for a week, something me, Anna, and Ike took turns doing during the summer. It was our getaway to a life beyond the sheltered borders of our village. In some ways, it was a total culture shock for us, but very exciting nonetheless.

Usually Dick and Helen would come on a Sunday and take one of us to stay with them for a week. It was finally my turn, but Sunday came and went and Dick and Helen did not come. I was very disappointed. Monday came and we did all the laundry, and then... there they were! After a wonderful visit and Mom's good cooking, I asked Mom if I could go. She hesitated, even when I mentioned that the heaviest work of the week had been done. She said it wasn't the work, but wouldn't say more. Finally she agreed to let me go, but before we left she wanted us to sing... something we usually did when they were over. She requested the song "Tell it to Jesus." Even though

Dick hadn't brought his guitar this time, we all sang it together in our summer kitchen. Afterward, Mother actually gave me a hug—which was not the norm. When we drove off, she waved and waved. This waving was also unusual, and we all commented on it.

CHAPTER THREE
Sad Endings

As usual, I had a wonderful week at my sister's. Friday night came and with it bedtime prayers with my sister's kids. As I listened to my young nephew say his prayers, he got to the "If I should die before I wake" part and something stabbed me right there. I had a hard time getting to sleep that night.

At two o'clock, the phone rang. Something was very wrong back home: Mom was not waking up! According to my sister, when I first heard this I just screamed and screamed, saying, "I should have stayed home... I should have stayed home!" She tried to reassure me as we bundled up all the kids and drove in silence back to Reinland.

I was in denial. The whole way, I tried to keep up a positive mental chatter: "Mom probably just fainted. I fainted once. She'll be okay. She was okay when we left on Monday..." But my sister and her husband didn't reply. They sensed it was more serious than that.

When we entered the village of my home, an eerie darkness seemed to envelop us... I wished I could escape, but the little Volkswagen into which we had piled the three sleepy and now very subdued children just kept on towards its dismal destination. I sensed that something was very wrong, but I tried one more hopeful comment: "See, there's Anna and Ike on the porch... they're not even crying. Therefore, everything must be okay."

But it all fell on deaf ears as we got out of the car and discovered the horrible truth: our mother had died! Anna and Ike were in shock. Not only was Anna the one to discover Mom as she died, but Ike and her had had to go for help... and this in a beat-up old truck which was dysfunctional, to say the least. Not to mention that Ike was only thirteen years old!

We came into the dark house with only the small lamps to light the way and found our Mom, motionless in her bed. Dad was beside himself with grief. Dick and Helen had to be the strong ones for all of us... which they were, as always. We all felt so lost. A doctor and a policeman, along with our brothers Abe and Bill, were on their way in two separate cars. But then they had an accident. The first driver was the policeman and he wasn't paying close enough attention to our brother's instructions in regards to the quick turn at the bottom of the hill. Because of this lack of attention, the doctor behind them crashed into their car. They had to abandon the damaged car and continue towards Reinland.

The doctor was so shaken up that Dick had to go to Warman to get another doctor, so that Mom could be pronounced legally dead.

The cause of Mom's death was difficult to assess; it seemed that she had just died peacefully in her sleep. The doctor noted, however, that she had been on heart medication, and it was cited as the reason for her sudden death.

Anna had woken up after hearing Mom groan. These groans were followed by quick gasps of breath, so she got up to investigate. She couldn't get Mom to wake up; when she lifted her arm, there was no response. She then alerted Dad, who at first objected to all the fussing until he too realized that something was seriously wrong with Mom.

I experienced great guilt in the years that followed my mother's death, always thinking I was partially to blame. I hadn't been there to help her more, and so I thought she must have been overworked. However, many years later, I was able to address this issue through a program called "Steps to Freedom." The program was introduced in our local church in Neepawa by a couple from Winnipeg. After group teaching, we each had the option to go through it privately with the facilitator and two prayer partners. We had to set aside a full day, during which the facilitator guided us through different events and times in our lives. During this time, we asked God to reveal areas in our lives that He wanted us to repent of, be healed from, and generally be set free from in order to live a fruitful and spiritually mature life.

The Lord revealed to me that it had been His plan for me to be absent from home at the time of my mother's death. You see, if I'd been there, I would not have allowed Anna to go and investigate Mom's groaning. Even when Helen was still home, Mom often made groaning noises at night and we older ones never gave it much thought; she was always okay. Anna, as the youngest, however, had never heard this and naturally went to investigate and found her just as she died. If I'd been home, we would possibly not have found her until morning. How great would have been my guilt then! I would always have considered myself responsible, thinking, *If we had only investigated, we might have saved her!* What a freedom I finally experienced during this session... God is so good!

After my mom died, women from the village came and sat in silence in the living room (our parent's bed was in one corner of this large room). I was weeping inconsolably and must have gotten too loud because I was asked to be quiet. I felt so alone and made my way outside. The rooster crowed, which made me very angry—how could everything carry on as usual when my whole life was turned upside-down? My younger sister said later that her consolation was that Jesus had to be coming back very soon; it was otherwise impossible to carry on. My consolation came in the form of songs in my heart which God gave to shelter me from more anger.

Someone tried to console our father by telling him that at least Mom's face would not be forgotten, as his youngest daughter looked exactly like her. I looked at Anna as they took Mom's body away and realized for the first time that she really did look like Mom.

My aunties noticed that Mom had actually made two kinds of soup, more than would normally be needed, and that the chicken noodle soup was actually turning sour because the weather had been so hot. They wondered if she had known she would soon be going "home" and tried to prepare for the many people that would be coming. She often told us as children that she wouldn't be with us much longer, but we always dismissed it, thinking that's what all mothers said.

Later that day, as we prepared to go to bed, our brother Bill had devotions with us. He read from 1 Thessalonians 5:16–18: *"Rejoice evermore. Pray without ceasing. In every thing give thanks: for this is the will of God in Christ Jesus concerning you"* (KJV). At first I was appalled; this was not the right time for this Scripture. But Bill also shared challenging words of insight for us: "God must trust us to continue following Him despite this extreme hardship. We should consider it a great honour to be so trusted." This became my inspiration to keep going: I would not succumb to self-pity, but take up the challenge before me. God would take care of us. I, for one, wanted to see and experience how He would do so!

Our final question that night was, would we be dishonouring Mom if we now started going to the Evangelical church? We didn't come up with an answer and wearily prepared for bed.

We were offered sleeping pills by the doctor; I took half of one, but my younger sister said no. This refusal was very significant considering the natural sleep and God-given dream she was to have that night. She saw Mom in heaven watching us attend the Evangelical church and clapping her hands for joy. Our sweet little Anna was given such a beautiful dream to set all our minds at ease.

But this ease only lasted until the funeral: there, during the sermon, the minister made reference to our brothers leaving the church, which had brought stress to our mother. Although subtle, none of us missed the implication: we were partly to blame for our mother's early death—she was only fifty-five.

My two friends from high school came to the funeral and tried to comfort me. After the funeral, others living outside our village did their best for us: sewing beautiful matching skirts for Anna and me at Easter time, and doing many other acts of kindness to lighten our grief. There was not much comfort coming from our little village; the words from the pulpit seemed to silence the comfort that might other-wise have come. I remember sitting in our old truck with Dad and Ike, reminiscing and sharing our lonely feelings. It was perhaps one of the few moments of genuine closeness we shared with our dad during this time.

I was therefore more than happy to resume my other life at high school where I had the understanding and acceptance of my friends. I still studied hard. However, my marks plummeted and I was exempted in only five of the eight subjects in my Grade Ten year. I was having a difficult year, to say the least. I was in charge of the cooking, cleaning, laundry, and everything else, it seemed, and all this without the help of electricity or running water. Ike was very helpful, always bringing in firewood and hauling water for the washing. Anna, now eleven, also had to grow up fast and do her share.

There were times when I was very discouraged. On one occasion, my brother Henry wanted to work on a motor which he had brought into the house. I could envision nothing but a greasy mess, and so I objected. He objected even more strongly, and I felt he would pull rank and get his way. (Seniority seemed to have a lot of sway in our culture, and Henry was two years older than me). I went to my room crying, seriously considering suicide. I wondered if I could slam the window down hard enough with my head stuck through it! I was so overwhelmed! Soon, however, there was a knock on my door and my father assured me that the motor had been removed from the kitchen. I felt greatly comforted by my father's intervention and this encouraged me to keep going.

Dad also tried to help me when I insisted on going to high school on even the bitterly cold days. During the winter, the road past our yard was not accessible to the school bus, and I had to walk a long way to a farm where the bus would pick me up. The people there had a daughter going as well and always invited me in to wait for the bus. My father didn't like me walking that far in such cold weather, so he went to the neighbours and borrowed a "stone boat" and a horse. This was normally used to haul manure out to the field. Although it was very embarrassing for me to be sitting on this stone boat as we passed through the village, I knew my father was taking care of me the best way he knew how.

However, he couldn't do much to make our first Christmas without Mom like the ones we'd had before. Adding to the sad fact that Mom was missing, I came down with a very painful ear infection, waking up Christmas morning knowing that this was definitely the worst Christmas of my life. Later, Abe and his wife Mary came and promptly took me to Warman, to visit Dick and Helen. They took me to a doctor, where I got medicine to alleviate the pain. It was encouraging to have older siblings looking out for us.

Another encouragement came as we started attending the Evangelical church. The choir director/youth leader came to pick us up on Friday nights, and on Sunday mornings the Sunday School teacher came and took us to church. This was the highlight of our week, and we found comfort and support there. It was that first spring after our mom died that Ike, Anna, and I started singing as a trio. The church really encouraged us in this, calling us "The Derksen Trio." We thrived on the love and acceptance they gave us, and the Lord used these precious people to bring healing to our lonely hearts.

Our father, however, was again failing mentally. He had been in the mental hospital prior to Mom's death and had just recovered before she died. Now he was unable to be the head of the home and to direct and support us as teenagers. Instead, we were now worrying about him.

A year after our mom's death, we sold our house in Reinland and moved to Warman, where Dick and Helen lived. But it was a very small house. We were used to our very large Mennonite-style home, with a summer kitchen connecting it to the barn. It was difficult now to adjust to just two small rooms. However, Dad built an addition and it even had electricity. We had our own well and could easily get water for laundry.

The sad thing was that Dad had to go back to the mental hospital for a few months. I had a boyfriend at this time, and it wasn't good for us four teenagers to live without a chaperone. This prompted our brother Bill to come and live with us, moving out of Saskatoon where he was a student at the university. He commuted with our brother-in-law Dick, who worked in the city as a mechanic.

Bill brightened our lives considerably. He introduced us to classical music, even entrusting us with much of his record collection when he left. He even tried to give Ike and myself violin lessons. It never clicked for me, but Ike went on to be an accomplished violinist just like big brother Bill.

When Dad came back home, he was much improved. We finally had some normalcy as teenagers: friends, a good high school, a good church, and most of all we lived close to our sister Helen! We did a lot of babysitting for them and Helen continued to do a lot of sewing for us. Dick often took us to Saskatoon for shopping as well as to my job; I worked at Kresge's lunch counter on Saturdays. Even though we no longer had our mother, we were very blessed and supported in our new surroundings.

CHAPTER FOUR

Manitoba Beginnings

What was I to do after high school? University was out of the question, as my math marks were too low... I was no longer the A student I had been in Grade Nine. I wanted to go to Bible school, but which one was I going to attend? By this time, I'd had two boyfriends, both nice Christian guys. The first one was from the village, a nephew of Dick's. But when I started high school, I knew he would not belong in my world. Even though he was a sincere Christian, he did not feel called to leave the conservative Mennonite life behind, as I knew I must. In high school, I met another Christian guy, but it was not meant to be.

So when I left for Steinbach Bible School in Manitoba after graduation, I was definitely leaving this whole "guy thing" alone. I just wanted to study God's Word and eventually go to Teacher's College to become a teacher!

In the fall of 1964, I packed my bags and, together with my cousin, made my way via rail to the wonderful land of promise... Steinbach Bible School! When I arrived, I felt I had come home. The staff and students accepted me and made me feel so welcome. How could school be this much fun? I shared a spacious dorm room with two roommates, one of whom was definitely the big sister type. The food was terrific and I didn't have to cook it! (I gained ten pounds by Christmas time, which was okay, because I had been underweight until then). And the courses were wonderful. Best of all, *there was no math!* In my second year, my brother Bill even came to teach as a music instructor. Imagine my thrill, having my own brother teach me music and being under his direction in choir.

I felt so free, so young, so loved and accepted. Most of all, I felt very blessed by God. I remembered my fervent prayers for a new life where I could be with fellow believers in an Evangelical setting. It seemed clearer to me now how the purposes of God could unfold from tragedy to beauty. My mother herself had sensed that I was not meant to stay in Reinland, but how sad I felt knowing that when she was taken home, it opened the way for this to happen. My prayers were answered, but at what cost?

First-year students weren't allowed to date, and I was okay with that. No guys for me! Difficult as that might be to substantiate, I had not come to Bible school for that reason. I did have ambitious plans, after all: three years of Bible school and then I was on to Teacher's College. My older siblings expected this of me, or so I thought at the time.

God had even more wonderful plans in store. My roommate kept bragging about her cousin, who happened to be in her third-year class. I paid little attention to her daily humorous highlights in regards to "Cousin Ruben." She probably had meant to interest the other Grade Twelve roommate. Again, God was doing the matchmaking here.

Eventually it came to the point where I ended up meeting this *person*. And he was scary! Even though she had tried to explain who he was, I had never attempted to identify him in the Bible school crowd. But this particular evening, we both needed a ride to "The Messiah" choir practice uptown. This was no problem, my roommate explained. Ruben would be more than happy to give us a ride in his little VW... more than happy, indeed! When she asked him, he gave her a dreadful scowl and a resounding "No"! She shook with laughter while I shook with fear! She brushed him aside as we piled into his little car. "He's always teasing," she remarked. But I was seriously wondering if we'd get a ride home. I realized later that he did have a smile... perhaps he just needed the right woman to bring it out!

A few weeks later, his sister, whom I knew as a friend even before I met him, invited my roommate and me, along with another lonely dormer, for Sunday dinner. And guess who was there? Her brother Ruben, of course. He was his usual self—dry humour and serious face all the way through. At one point, he was asked by his sister to get pickles from downstairs, to which he again replied with a resounding "No!" She merely said please, and off he went for the pickles as if it was all his idea. He was asked to say the grace, which he did, messing it up on purpose, all with a straight face. My roommate kept laughing; she so enjoyed his antics, but I still wasn't quite sure.

He tried to keep out of our way when it was clean-up time, lying down on the living room couch until we were finished. When we came into the living room, I saw him slouching there. Having lost all my fear of this tall handsome guy, I now teased him about his laziness and threw a cushion at him. With a totally serious face, he whizzed it right back at me. I believe that started the spark of love between us!

The next morning, Ruben greeted me at school with an enthusiastic hello, to which I returned a rather casual greeting. I wasn't sure I wanted him or anyone else to think there was something between us.

Finally he had the courage to ask me out. I still wasn't sure, and thought that I could bow out on the "no dating in first-year" policy. Ruben was a third-year student. The dean of women, however, didn't hesitate to give me permission, so I told Ruben yes. He was overjoyed.

That's when I began to think about this more seriously. We went out to a concert in Winnipeg, and I felt totally at peace about the relationship. We continued to "see" each other. As he walked me to the dorm, sat beside me on choir trips, treated me to peanuts and chocolate bars after the library hour, and talked to me as he swept the music room where I was "practicing," I gradually realized He was God's man for me. Ruben made me feel so special, so accepted, and so loved. I found myself falling hopelessly in love with this Prince Charming.

However, I went back to Saskatchewan to work for the summer in the city of North Battleford. Along with several other young people from different Bible schools across Canada, I lived in a house owned by a pastor and his wife. Most of us worked in the seven-hundred-bed mental hospital there. We had great times together under the supervision of the couple. We were paired up for cooking the meals and doing chores, and were also involved in outreach and church activities. When Ruben came to visit, he was well-accepted. However, his visits were too short and not often enough; we were so lonesome. Finally, it was time to return to Manitoba for my second year of Bible School... and to Ruben!

During February of my second year, he asked me to marry him. Without any hesitation, I said yes! Plans were made for a summer wedding on August 27, 1966.

First, however, I went on a trio tour with another two Bible school friends, my future sister-in-law (who was the pianist), and a minister from the Bible school. We toured all over Manitoba, going as far north as Thompson, and we had a very enjoyable time. There was only one thing missing: Ruben!

After the tour, it was back to Saskatchewan to work until our wedding day. Ruben came to Saskatoon at the end of June, after finishing his Grade Twelve. He had already completed his three years of Bible school. My older sister helped me choose a wedding gown, but after that they moved to Pambrun, where Dick would be taking Bible school training. I had little experience planning a wedding and had only been to one "white wedding" the previous summer—when Bill married Maryrose Reimer in Steinbach. They were in Saskatoon now as well, and so helpful with the music. My bridesmaid helped me shop for my trousseau and decorate the church. My brother Ike was roommates with Ruben, and Anne (no longer Anna) was my roommate in a house a few blocks away. Both of them were very involved in helping with the wedding.

My brother Abe and his wife Mary went to great lengths to help: Mary made our wedding cake. I still have the recipe and make this fruit cake every Christmas! We all had some fun times together that summer—going boating on the lake, having picnics, and just hanging out. Everyone really liked Ruben. He was my dream come true, and I knew God had led me to Steinbach Bible School partly to meet him. As I said the next year in my grad speech, "I'm glad I came to SBI, and so is Ruben!"

The wedding day dawned bright and clear and I was so ready for it, except for one glitch: I had come down with laryngitis! Thankfully the wedding didn't start until 4:30 p.m., by which time I was able to speak. Because my family and I were not familiar with the proceedings of a "white wedding," no one had been assigned to give me away. So, as I walked down the aisle to Maryrose's organ refrains of "Trumpet Voluntaire," my bouquet of red roses was shaking. I remember feeling like Cinderella: *Once I get to the front where my handsome Prince Charming is waiting, I will truly live "happily ever after"!*

Ruben had planned our honeymoon. We had a blissful week in Banff, Alberta. Then we headed back to Saskatoon where Ruben was committed to working another month at the mechanics shop where he had started at the end of June. I had worked full-time in a nursing home as a nurse's aide, but after the wedding I continued on a casual basis.

But we couldn't wait to get back to our life in Steinbach. We moved at the end of September, and I resumed my studies at SBI while Ruben worked as a mechanic. This was a year of adjustments and joys, as it is for most newlyweds. Ruben was in the same church conference

as I was, which gave us even more in common. We soon found ourselves involved in activities and friendships at the EMMC (Evangelical
Mennonite Mission Conference) church in Steinbach.

My third year of Bible school was going well. I had purposefully
taken extra courses in the second year to make this year easier. Now,
I was almost bored! Graduation was in April and already a few of my
married fellow grads were expecting their first child. Everyone was
watching me, thinking I must be pregnant, too, especially because
I had gained some weight and was wearing an empire waist dress I
had made myself. Alas, it was not so. Even though we weren't actually
ready at that time, had we known what was ahead, we would have
been alarmed at the seeming bleakness of our future.

While our friends were looking forward to their babies arriving, I
was finding part-time jobs to keep me busy. Ruben and I hadn't figured
out exactly what it was that God wanted us to do, so Ruben worked
for a farmer that first summer. Since farming was his greatest love, we
found a small acreage just outside Steinbach, which we bought with
the help of a loan from Ruben's dad. They had sold their farm in Rosen-
feld and now lived in Steinbach as well. His dad often came to help.
Ruben also worked full-time in town as a welder while I was "stuck"
out on our acreage. Eventually, I managed to get my driver's license so
that I could go to town.

CHAPTER FIVE
No New Beginnings

I was taking a walk through the snow at our little acreage near Steinbach. The bright sun made the white snow almost dazzle. What a cozy place, I thought, for a young couple so in love, as we were. I was filled with gratitude as I realized again how the Lord had led us together. We were so happy, life was so wonderful. Except there was an ache in my heart... a yearning, as yet unfulfilled, for a new life to complete our happiness. The longing for a "baby Ruben" came while we were watching a story on television about a young couple who were desperately trying to have children. I could just picture a miniature Ruben with beautiful black hair and long, curly eyelashes. (I must have gotten missed when eyelashes were given out; mine weren't visible without mascara!) I longed so much to hold him—or her— but... there seemed to be no sign of him.

Now, as I was trudging through the snow, I asked God why. After I'd poured out my heart to Him, I returned to our winterized cottage-style house and noticed again the motto on the living room wall: *"Delight thyself also in the Lord; and he shall give thee the desires of thine heart. Commit thy way unto the Lord; trust also in him; and he shall bring it to pass"* (Psalm 37:4–5, KJV). This brought me a measure of peace and comfort. I had thought, however, that my journey to motherhood would be a quick, nine-month jaunt like my friends around me. Little did I realize the detours, bumps, bends, and ruts I would encounter on my journey.

Eventually I went to the doctor, who told me there was no reason why I couldn't have children. But he also suggested that Ruben come in. He did, and here we found out the devastating truth—there would never be a miniature Ruben. He was sterile and we were advised to adopt. This was a huge blow from which it would be very difficult to recover. Procreation is a powerful dynamic in life, and to know it cannot happen takes you off the path of "normal" into a confusing whirlpool of the unknown. The agony and pain of natural childbirth is hard, but it is natural and naturally rewarded. The agony and frustration of seeing natural procreation wiped away as never to be achieved has no rewards with it, and left us with a feeling of emptiness, a sense of being trapped. To say the least, our path would be very different from that of our friends.

For one thing, we felt very lonely; there didn't seem to be anyone else in our plight, so when we tried to share it we got nothing but pity. But we didn't want pity, we needed answers! What should we do now? For me, there was no answer other than a baby Ruben, and that could not happen now. Ruben broached the topic of adoption, but I wasn't ready. However, we prayed about it and tried to trust God with all this. One day, I asked God to give me a sign about whether or not we should adopt. A little while after this prayer, my new neighbour, whom I'd never met before, came to the door with her two children. She explained how they were her special, adopted children whom the Lord had blessed them with. She seemed very happy and I knew this was God's sign to me.

CHAPTER SIX

Adoption Beginnings

In July of 1968, we applied for adoption, praying that God would choose the little girl that He wanted us to have. It was an exciting time of preparation—sewing little dresses, knitting sweaters and booties. But it was also a gruelling time of answering all kinds of questions never put to natural parents. We were walking a very different path, indeed.

We didn't know exactly what else to do in preparation. So like with everything else, Ruben bought a book—a book on adoption. This helped a lot, and when three months later we received word from the agency to come and meet our little girl, we were absolutely overjoyed! The book said you wouldn't be able to take the baby home right away; it would just be a meeting time. Therefore, we didn't take any baby clothes, just our excited selves and a name we had picked out for her.

The social worker seated us and then left the room to bring out our baby. A beautiful, five-and-a-half-week-old baby girl was placed into my arms and we named her Melissa Shelene. (Later my older sister said she knew why I had chosen that name *Melissa*: when I was very little, Mother used to call me *kjleena Meleeza*, Low German for "little Melissa.")

Melissa seemed a little wary as she looked up at us, and why wouldn't she be? First she didn't get to be with her natural mommy, then she got taken away from her foster mommy, and now she was like, "Excuse me, but who are you?" However, she seemed very relaxed as we admired her, and yes, we took her home right away! (The book was wrong on that one!) We were so happy to finally have a baby! Our families were very happy for us as well, knowing how hard all this had been for us.

A new baby in the house, wow! Life was so different. A friend of mine had had her little girl just three weeks prior, and she became my mentor in my new role. She was a nurse and had worked in the maternity ward a lot, so she was very confident and optimistic. I'd had a lot of experience babysitting my nieces and nephews, but this was different.

When we first got Melissa, the many changes and busy nights were hard on me as a light sleeper. Often I couldn't get back to sleep after feedings, so occasionally I took a sleeping pill that the doctor had prescribed for me. One night, Ruben took his turn feeding Melissa her bottle and I was supposed to be fast asleep. However, he and the baby were fast asleep in the living room chair while I and my sleeping pill were wide awake, wondering if they were all right!

I seemed to experience extreme highs and lows. I didn't know what was happening. Melissa continued to be wary of us, it seemed, and brought out our own insecurities and self-doubts.

Since that time, we have studied and researched the whole adoption procedure and how it affects the child. Studies show that babies can sense things already in the womb. When they are to be given up for adoption, they may feel robbed and lied to; they will not be nurtured by the natural mother who is carrying them and their heritage will be "stolen" from them as well. Thus, they come with their own rejection issues and may even have a tendency toward lying and stealing.

We didn't understand this at the time, and sometimes I felt defeated in my role as a mother. I blamed myself a lot and felt I just wasn't getting this motherhood thing. Ruben, however, blessed me by leaving a bookmark in his Bible at Proverbs 31—the description of the Virtuous Woman. Along the border, he had printed my name! Wow! That was the gift that encouraged me to find answers and get away from guilt. As well, we met other adoptive parents who were going through the same struggles, so we realized we were actually "normal" after all!

Gradually things got better; we stopped taking everything so personally. Melissa was a very smart, talkative, and active little girl who loved nothing better than to meet new people. She would ask store clerks personal questions and I would have to tell them they didn't need to answer. She was so cute and adored by all. She was also very musical and right on pitch when she sang. And sing she did, often making up her own songs, telling me to "sing with me, you know it!"

When Melissa was two years old, we started to pray about what the Lord would have us do. We knew Ruben wouldn't be welding in town all his life. Already in Bible school, we had committed ourselves to be available for missions, if that was what God wanted for us. But where, how, and what would that look like? Ruben loved welding; maybe he could teach it. We applied to Red River Community College for Industrial Arts teacher training. We also applied to Village Missions for short-term missions work. They did not have anything in short-term missions, it turned out, but the college sent a letter of acceptance. Our course was clear; we knew that whatever and wherever God called us, we would be His missionaries.

CHAPTER SEVEN
Winnipeg Beginnings

We moved to Winnipeg where Ruben started working as a milkman, because he wouldn't be able to start college until the following term. In September, he started his training at Red River Community College. We needed an income, of course, so we moved to a large apartment complex where we took on the manager/caretaker job. This proved a very challenging task, since Ruben wasn't around most days to chip off the ice on the parking area ramp. I had to do the cleaning, sometimes taking little Melissa with me, and at other times I did it while she was sleeping, going back constantly to check on her.

Ruben was doing very well at school, so we kept struggling on. Anne and her new husband Ron (she had married her sweetheart from Bible school as well) moved into the main floor of our building, into a one-bedroom next to us. My brother Ike moved into a bachelor's suite on the sixth floor. Even though all the floors looked alike, Melissa always knew which floor was Uncle Ike's.

We had great times there. The swimming pool was our responsibility as well, but we as managers could use it after hours—and we often did. My siblings and I had never really learned to swim, so this was a good learning opportunity for us. We were also able to use the party room, where we had great birthday celebrations with family and friends.

Our time there came to an end when Ruben's older brother and sister-in-law were killed in a car crash. The owner of the building graciously gave us leave of our duties. We couldn't understand why nobody was coming to our door, but it was because there was a note there directing tenant enquiries to the neighbouring apartment manager. These two apartment blocks were connected by a tunnel and they both belonged to the same agency.

We moved to a rental house shortly after that. It was an older house that had been fixed up. It had an electric fireplace in the living room and French doors that led into the dining room, complete with hardwood floors throughout. The kitchen was large and bright, and we really liked it. The owners lived upstairs and were kind and generous.

Melissa was three years old that summer and I felt I had to get a job to help my husband through his second year of college. I was hired as a nurse's aide at the Children's Hospital (now part of the Health Sciences Centre). The neighbour across the street offered to babysit, so we started off that fall with me working full-time and Ruben a full-time student. Melissa seemed to adjust all right, but after a while we did switch babysitters, to someone from our church.

Working on the infectious diseases ward was hard on my hands, as we had to wash continuously with abrasive soaps, causing a bad breakout of eczema on my hands. I applied for a job in the hospital pharmacy instead, where I worked as a clerk. It was a very organized and well-run place. I really enjoyed it. We carpooled with a couple from our area; he was taking the same course as Ruben at Red River College and she was a nurse at the Children's Hospital. They became very good friends.

After Ruben's graduation, he got a job teaching in Jefferson Junior High School in Winnipeg. During this time, we prayed about having more children. Although we were considering adoption again, we still had a yearning for natural children. When we heard there was a new fertility clinic started at what was then the General Hospital, Ruben asked for an appointment and went several times. I remember waiting for him after work, anxious to know if there was any possibility of us having natural children. He finally came out and gave the grim verdict: I would never be pregnant by him. If I wanted to be pregnant, it would have to be artificial insemination by a different donor! It was a sobering ride home. We both chastised ourselves for having fostered such high hopes in the medical field. Never would I want to be pregnant with anybody's baby but Ruben's; it was the miniature Ruben I still longed for!

Night after night, I poured out my unfulfilled longings to God, pleading with Him to at least make me completely content with adoption, like my friend in Steinbach had been. Finally, I sensed the comforting voice of my Heavenly Father, assuring me that there would be natural children in the future and our longings would be fulfilled!

The verse He had given me before we adopted came back again: *"Delight thyself also in the Lord... and he shall bring it to pass"* (Psalm 37:4–5, KJV). I was at peace after that. My sister Anne couldn't believe it. Not even Ruben could believe it!

Ruben didn't want to stay in the city, so he faithfully looked in the paper for Industrial Arts teaching positions outside of Winnipeg. He finally found one in the little town of Neepawa, an hour away from Brandon. He also encouraged me to go to the community college in Brandon, so I registered as a student for their Social Services course.

We moved to an apartment in Brandon, which was close to my college and only a block from Melissa's first school. Each day I'd walk her to school and then continue on to my college. She and I would walk to school while Ruben commuted to Neepawa in our brand new Mazda. I learned a lot in my course and became more confident as an adoptive mom.

We were also on a spiritual quest at this time. While in Winnipeg, we were affected by the revival that was happening there. We started reading books on the baptism of the Holy Spirit, a term very foreign to us. Even though we had read how Jesus promised the Holy Spirit to His disciples, we had received no real teaching on this until now. We began to see that God had more to give, and we wanted to experience all He had for us. It was enlightening for us to know that His Spirit living within us could powerfully change the way we lived our Christian lives, giving us more power, love, and hope as we yielded fully to Him. It seemed we had lived so much of our Christian lives by relying on our own feeble strength.

While in Brandon, we attended the Alliance church, and I was reminded each Sunday that God was going to do a miracle in our lives. The sign on the pulpit read: "Expect a Miracle." I was so sure it would happen that I even told some of my fellow students that someday we would have natural children. Amazingly, they believed me and asked me to keep them posted!

After my graduation a year later, we moved to Neepawa where we bought a new house close to Ruben's school. Now Ruben could walk to school, which was a relief for him after driving two hours every day the year before! Melissa was in Grade One and I had a job at the local hospital as ward clerk. However, I was not content there, as I wanted to work in the field I had just studied. After about two weeks, I resigned; I was being considered for a job as a daycare coordinator. This, however, proved to be a premature decision: they hired a teacher, since it was more of a preschool setting. I was okay with that, but now found myself alone at home with nothing to do, which was quite a change from how busy my life had been before.

CHAPTER EIGHT

Holy Spirit Beginnings

I realized this was a God-given time to continue my search for more of the Lord. One day, I sat at my kitchen table and asked Him to baptize me with His Holy Spirit. I felt impressed to check my heart for anything I might need to give up in order for Him to do this. Immediately my daily rendezvous with my favourite TV soap came to mind. Oh yes, *As the World Turns* had better not turn without me! I couldn't believe that God was really asking me to give up this little thing! I asked Him to send me an interruption at 2:30 p.m., the time when the show was to start. I always hated when people phoned or came to the door at this time!

It was two o'clock when I started praying, opening myself up to receive more of His Holy Spirit and His gift of tongues. A scripture came to mind from the Gospel of Luke:

> Which of you fathers, if your son asks for a fish, will give
> him a snake instead? Or if he asks for an egg, will give him
> a scorpion? If you then, though you are evil, know how to
> give good gifts to your children, how much more will your
> Father in heaven give the Holy Spirit to those who ask
> Him! (Luke 11:11–13)

As I prayed, I became very aware of the cross and what Jesus had
done for me. I received a few "words" in tongues, but I wasn't focusing on that. Instead, I was filled with a release of joy that I'd never had
before... God was truly visiting me. Then, I opened my eyes and it was
2:30! I remembered my show. Was God going to send me an interruption? Just as I got up to turn on the TV, the phone rang and I jumped! It
was Ruben telling me he would be a bit late. After I hung up, I laughed
and laughed! God *had* sent me an interruption. He was real and He had
filled me with a new joy! And He had a sense of humour! When Ruben
came home, he knew immediately that something had happened to
me. Not long after that, he experienced it, too.

Several Anglicans under the leadership of their pastor were seeking renewal in our community and we fellowshipped with them every
Tuesday night. We were gently mentored and encouraged in our new
walk, but we continued to attend the Baptist church where we tried to
walk out what we experienced. We learned the hard way that rather
than blurt out our experience, we needed to refrain from sharing it unless we felt there was an openness to receive it.

CHAPTER NINE
Hannah Beginnings

G od began speaking to us about exercising faith in regards to natural children, so we read the story of Hannah and Samuel as found in 1 Samuel:

> There was a certain man... whose name was Elkanah... He had two wives; one was called Hannah and the other Peninnah. Peninnah had children, but Hannah had none.
>
> Year after year this man went up from his town to worship and sacrifice to the Lord Almighty at Shiloh... Whenever the day came for Elkanah to sacrifice, he would give portions of the meat to Peninnah and to all her sons and daughters. But to Hannah he gave a double portion because he loved her, and the Lord had closed her womb. And because the Lord had closed her womb, her rival [Peninnah] kept provoking her in order to irritate her.

This went on year after year. Whenever Hannah went up to the house of the Lord, her rival provoked her till she wept and would not eat...

In bitterness of soul Hannah wept much and prayed to the Lord. And she made a vow, saying, "O Lord Almighty, if you will only look upon your servant's misery and remember me, and not forget your servant but give her a son, then I will give him to the Lord for all the days of his life..."

As she kept on praying to the Lord, Eli [the priest] observed her mouth. Hannah was praying in her heart and her lips were moving but her voice was not heard. Eli thought she was drunk and said to her, "How long will you keep on getting drunk? Get rid of your wine!"

"Not so, my lord," Hannah replied, "I am a woman who is deeply troubled. I have not been drinking wine or beer; I was pouring out my soul to the Lord. Do not take your servant for a wicked woman; I have been praying here out of my great anguish and grief."

Eli answered, "Go in peace, and may the God of Israel grant you what you have asked of Him..."

So in the course of time Hannah conceived and gave birth to a son. She named him Samuel, saying, "Because I asked the Lord for him." (1 Samuel 1:1–7, 10–17, 20)

We read this story and felt it would be our prayer, too. But we wondered if we should be praying this way. Our old beliefs were still casting doubts. However, the Lord was gracious. The next day was Sunday and our Baptist minister's sermon was on the story of Hannah and Samuel! We looked at each other and knew it was God's confirmation to us.

The Anglicans had an annual Holy Spirit conference which we'd already attended once. This year, we were asked to be prayer counsellors. The night before the conference, I was again burdened with a longing for natural children and went to pray in our bedroom. I came back, announcing to Ruben, "When God blesses us with a natural child, we will name him Samuel to show the world that God still does miracles today!"

The next day, there seemed to be many obstacles to keep us from going to the conference. I was anxiously looking at the clock, waiting for 4:30, which was quitting time for me. I was working as a secretary in the agricultural office in our town. However, many clients were coming in to see the boss and I knew I'd have responsibilities to attend to after they left. It looked like I'd be working late, but I tried to pray and just relax. Calm and joy came over me and I was able to do some important work in that next half-hour with precision and efficiency. The blessing came when the boss offered to take the money to the post office himself, which he didn't usually do since it was my job. I praised the Lord as I left, thinking I'd have time for those last-minute details at home.

However, obstacle number two was all laid out for me when I stepped outside, expecting to jump into my waiting "taxi." Well, the taxi was waiting, but the taxi driver (my husband) was nowhere to be seen. The taxi assistant (our sweet daughter) informed me that he was in some store, getting something, and she had forgotten what it was! I began stewing and fretting, intermittently trying to say, "Praise the Lord." Rather unsuccessfully, I might add.

I ran into the nearest store, found he wasn't there, then jumped back into my motionless taxi. My frustration turned to anger. The nerve of my husband! Well, I'd go home without him. If he had things to do uptown, I had *many* things to do at home. I was on the verge of carrying out this brash alternative, when I saw him *and* our pastor coming toward the car. My ruffled feathers smoothed down rather hurriedly—outwardly, at least. Inwardly, I was still seething when we got home.

Rather than walking in the peace I'd received earlier, I informed my darling husband of how he'd made me so frustrated. This didn't go over that well with my former taxi driver, and before we knew it we had created a "scene"—and not of the "scenic type," either! Needless to say, the minor details of preparation I'd been so anxious to attend to got substituted for some major unplanned ones. My organized thoughts were scattered disturbingly throughout the house and it took me a while to collect them. I was seriously considering not going at all, but thankfully God's gentle reminder of His ways came back to me. So after praying together, love and harmony were restored and I wondered what I'd been so upset about!

It was a very humbled Mari who went to the conference. All through the hearty praise and worship, I had feelings of regret. I certainly was not feeling worthy of being a prayer counsellor. When it was time for us to go and help in the ministry room, I could only pray that I wouldn't be a hindrance. As one person after another was prayed for, I kept trying to forgive myself and just look to Jesus.

One curly-haired woman sat down, asking us to pray that she'd have a safe pregnancy this time—she'd had several miscarriages. At that moment, something just went "thud" inside me and I actually had to sit down. A torrent of tears broke from my heart; people didn't seem to pay too much attention to me, except for my friend Grace, who was sitting next to me. She whispered, "Mari, behave yourself." She always got to me with her casual sense of humour, and I was able to collect myself as the rest prayed for this woman. I had been totally unprepared for that outburst, but maybe the woman's situation had triggered my own emotions.

At the end of the prayer session, people seemed to wait for me to sit in the "prayer chair." Ruben sensed it as well and saved the moment when he suggested we needed two chairs. He went on to explain that we couldn't have natural children but felt God wanted to change that for us.

When we sat down in the two chairs, I felt like a child about to receive another toy even though her room wasn't cleaned up yet. Everyone gathered around with such exuberance. The leader made remarks like, "Mark the calendar. You should see the results we get with this kind of request." And also, "Oh good, we get to pray over a man, too." As they started praying and praising God, I was overwhelmed with joy and gratitude. I had never dreamt that Jesus had planned this for us, especially after the way I'd acted earlier that afternoon. Big sobs came welling up again and by now Grace had completely given up on me "behaving myself!"

Some significant words of prophecy followed: "There will be children, one will be a Samuel." At that point, we knew that this was all God-directed. No one there knew of our "Hannah-type" prayer. So when we told the group about our faith journey so far, and that we'd actually read the story again just the night before, they responded with even more jubilation. On that note, the session ended and we returned to our room, full of faith and joy.

CHAPTER TEN

Samuel Beginnings

We walked in this faith euphoria for the next few weeks, fully expecting to be pregnant right away. However, when it didn't happen the first month, I realized we had to let God do this in His timetable, not ours. The next month was Easter, and we were having Ruben's family over. I was very excited about the whole message of Easter; I decorated our whole basement with crosses hanging from the ceiling that said "HE LIVES." It was a beautiful Easter celebration.

And then, suddenly, something was different. Our hopes were high as I made a trip to the doctor. Ruben was anxiously waiting for me when I came home, and I couldn't hide it any longer: "Yes Ruben, I am pregnant!"

It had happened over the Easter weekend. While I had been busy focusing on Jesus' beautiful sacrifice for us, He had been doing the miracle. After ten years of marriage, I was finally pregnant! It was April 1976. Needless to say, our joy and anticipation knew no bounds!

We tried to be down to earth and cautious in revealing our secret, but it was hard, very hard. Neither Ruben nor I had ever been pregnant before, so we were on cloud nine! Once in a while, one of us would be brought down to earth by a session of nausea. (Ruben never took his turn!) Melissa, age seven, was mostly up on cloud nine herself, but she did come up with some "down to earth" sneaky logic: "Now we won't know whether the baby will be a girl or a boy, will we?" You see, we had started procedures for adopting a baby boy, but she had wanted a baby sister!

You can imagine the excitement in the family. A real live miracle was happening right in our home! Even our relatives were now open to believing that miracles could happen in our day and age.

I was progressing well, although with much nausea, which I knew was normal. But somehow there was anxiety with it as well, for which I sought the Lord. He gave me this verse, and a round song to go with it: *"The angel of the Lord encamps around those who fear him and he delivers them"* (Psalm 34:7).[1] While at camp with our Anglican friends, I shared this song and asked them for prayer about the anxiety. It was a special time of unity and blessing for all of us. It was also a statement of God's protection during this pregnancy. Even though I didn't know what was coming, He did, and I could trust myself to His care. His angel was encamped around me. He wasn't just flitting by, doing an occasional

---

1   See music and lyrics at the back of the book.

check on me. He was *stationed* there for the long haul. At the same time, I sensed that this wasn't going to be an ordinary pregnancy; I needed to continue trusting Him.

We had prayed like Hannah: "Lord, grant us a child and we will give him back to you." For us, it wasn't a big deal... we would do the usual child dedication, right?

In Hannah's case, she intended to literally bring her son to the temple for God to use there. Her heart so longed for a child that she was willing to give him up just to have this longing satisfied. She had never had children before; maybe she didn't realize that her longing wouldn't end once she'd carried the child and given birth to it. After that, a mother wants to nourish and keep her child close. Perhaps she was so focused on fulfillment that she couldn't see anything else beyond that. However, God saw the sincerity of her heart and He knew that her longings would *not* end with the birth of her child. He knew that she would grow to love him, and the longer she had him the harder it would be to give him up.

This parallels Esau's hunger for Jacob's stew. The story is found in Genesis 27. Esau was so famished that he wanted his immediate need fulfilled. Jacob seemingly bribed him with the meal in exchange for Esau's birthright. At that point, the birthright was irrelevant; food was his imminent need and he gave in to Jacob. Later, of course, he deeply regretted his decision. But it was too late.

Going back to Hannah, though, after the birth of baby Samuel, she would have become fully aware of the great sacrifice she had committed herself to, but she still went through with her promise:

> After he was weaned, she took the boy with her, young as
> he was, along with a three-year-old bull, an ephah of flour
> and a skin of wine, and brought him to the house of the
> Lord at Shiloh.
>
> When they had slaughtered the bull, they brought the
> boy to Eli, and she said to him, "As surely as you live, my
> lord, I am the woman who stood here beside you praying to
> the Lord. I prayed for this child, and the Lord has granted
> me what I asked of him. So now I give him to the Lord. For
> his whole life he will be given over to the Lord."
>
> And he worshipped the Lord there. (1 Samuel 1:24–28)

This was just like Abraham, who spent so many years waiting for a son. Then, when that son arrived, he took him up the mountain to sacrifice him on an altar to God, at God's request. When his son Isaac asked, "Father, where is the lamb for the sacrifice?" Abraham answered, "God will provide." And what had he told Sarah about where he was taking their precious son? It wasn't just *his* son he was going to sacrifice on that altar. Isaac belonged to Sarah, too. Oh, the turmoil that must have gone on in his heart, all of which he had to hide from his sweet innocent boy who was probably so happy to be on this three-day worship trip with his daddy, not knowing what might befall him. What anguish that must have been for Abraham!

I often wonder why God asked this of Abraham. Perhaps it was simply a test of faith. The heathen nations at that time offered their sons and daughters to gods and threw them into the fire to appease them. This was not easy even for the ungodly; it's human nature for parents to love their children more than their own lives. God tested Abraham—would he give up his son out of love for his God?

God looks on the heart. He is looking for a pure and humble heart, one that can be tested to see whether there is true faith. He never takes advantage of it, but rewards it. He rewarded Hannah by giving her three more sons and two daughters. He rewarded Abraham. Just as he was about to take the knife to his son, bound firmly on the altar, a ram bleated in a bush nearby. The angel of God stopped Abraham, pointing out the ram as the sacrifice that God had provided.

In the story of Hannah, we read in 1 Samuel 2 that she worshipped and praised God. What woman could first give up the baby she had prayed and yearned for for such a long time, and then rejoice and praise God after she'd done it? It must have been God Himself that filled her heart with peace and gave her words of praise. He always takes care of us when we are willing to sacrifice for Him.

Just like He would take care of me.

When I was in my sixth month of pregnancy, I knew something was wrong; I had a three-day flu with a headache and high fever. The doctor could do little to control this. Was something wrong with the baby? I was confused and sought the Lord; this was supposed to be a miracle baby, so surely nothing would go wrong, right God? I remembered the verse from Psalm 37—*"The angel of the Lord encamps around those who fear him and he delivers them."* But God was reminding me of our promise. Would I be willing to give up my baby like Hannah did? It was a very clear but gentle question, almost as if He really was giving me this choice. I knew I had to respond.

Hesitantly, with tears running down my face, I raised my hands slowly as a symbol of surrendering this child. I did it... I gave my longed-for baby back to God. But oh, it was hard! My brother had said at the time of our mother's death that when God entrusts us with a hard experience, He expects us to look to Him and trust Him, which we should consider an honour. Also now, it was an honour to have been asked to do the same thing as Hannah. God would have to answer all those who were dubious about miracles in the first place and deal with the aftermath of a "no-show" miracle. All I had to do was trust in Him. He was much bigger than the picture I could see. He would have to take care of us.

It was the Thanksgiving weekend. I wasn't feeling too well, and was experiencing some cramping. Having never been pregnant before, I really didn't know what was happening. Was this just a Braxton-Hicks contraction that would go away, or was it just the baby moving? I had been in touch with Judith, my Anglican nurse friend, and she didn't want to scare me, I guess. At any rate, Ruben was uptown buying groceries for our Thanksgiving dinner. All of a sudden, I experienced a huge cramp and then made a dash to the bathroom. My water had broken and it didn't look healthy. I needed to get to the hospital, but how was I to get a hold of Ruben? This was 1976, long before cell phones. I panicked. Which store had Ruben gone to? I tried to call a store, then realized I was looking in the phone book under the wrong town altogether!

I thought I'd send Melissa on her bike, but as she started off I knew that was a bad idea, so I called her back. I regretted my panic, knowing how this was upsetting her. We were both in tears. She was an innocent child who understood only that something was very wrong, and she could do nothing to help. I kept saying, "Please don't cry, Melissa.

Jesus will take care of everything. He knows what He's doing." Many years later, she told us that she had thought I was dying!

Finally, I called my friend Judith, who tried to reassure me. She went off on her bicycle to find Ruben. He came shortly thereafter and confirmed what I had thought: things didn't look good. But he was not panicked. He called the hospital, giving all the necessary information, saying we were coming immediately. We took Melissa to Judith's and headed for the hospital.

When we got there, we were met by the doctor who'd seen me earlier. He seemed to be calm and tried to reassure me. I knew, however, that this was it—my miraculous pregnancy status would soon be over. As the nurse helped me out of my prized maternity clothes, I knew I would not be wearing them upon leaving. I cried with great sobs: "O God, I waited ten years for this baby. I don't want to lose it!"

The nurse was very understanding as she helped me into bed. As the water kept coming, they tried to reassure me that it could be replaced and that the needle they gave me would make the contractions give up and go away. My pregnancy might yet continue. The pastor now came and prayed with us, asking God to protect the baby. Deep in my heart, I knew that my baby was already in heaven with God, but I appreciated that he came immediately to encourage us.

CHAPTER ELEVEN

Samuel Endings

Ruben stayed with me all night, comforting me as best he could. We both felt God's peace, and managed to sleep intermittently. The Demerol had subdued the labour somewhat during the night, but in the morning it came back with full force. It was Sunday, October 10, 1976. We had actually been asked to share our testimony in church that Sunday in regards to this miracle in our lives. That obviously would not happen now.

I prayed that God would just take this day and fulfill His plans, keeping me in His care. I had no strength to pray any noble prayers; my basic cry was for help! All I could ask was that God would give me strength for whatever would come this day. I sensed that perhaps God had a different miracle in mind than we did, and this brought a measure of peace. The past six months seemed not as important as God's present workings.

The help I had prayed for came as the Lord gave me moment-by-moment strength. As the contractions intensified, all I thought of was staying above it. Then, when it was gone, I relaxed... content to live one moment at a time. His peace enveloped me.

Around noon, the contractions got very intense and I needed to push. They had put me in a private room with a nurse's aide to attend me. She turned out to be the silent type... neither of us seemed to know what was happening. But then I had to push and actually asked for the bedpan! (As I said, I didn't know what was happening, but I certainly wasn't going to make a mess!) At the next push, the baby was born, but not alive. The doctor and nurses appeared, whisking me off to the delivery room. They didn't want me to see my baby, but I insisted. She was well-formed but dark in colour, as she had been dead inside me for a couple of weeks, at least. And yes, she was a little girl whom we always would refer to as "Samuella."

I was devastated and in shock at the reality of not having a baby. At the same time, I was overwhelmed with awe and wonder at the new feelings of motherhood that I now experienced. I also felt confused and bereft... there was no baby to be the recipient of these feelings. It was all so new and wonderful, yet so incredibly sad. I missed my little baby. She was in a bottle of formaldehyde waiting to be sent to the lab, and I was here in my hospital bed, alone. Eventually I went to sleep for the night, very exhausted.

I woke up a few hours later. Immediately the reality of it all sunk in: *There is no baby!* The euphoria, excitement, and anticipation of the last few months were over! I fully expected the first waves of depression to come now that Ruben wasn't here and I was alone in the darkness of my hospital room.

But something—no, Someone—was coming to me. It was the very real Presence of the Lord. He was so real. I couldn't see Him, but I definitely felt Him there. And oh, the joy, love, and peace that radiated from Him to me! I felt so comforted. It was as if He was inviting me to ask Him questions, which I did: *Why did this happen? What will I do with all these wonderful new motherhood feelings? What do I do now?* And He answered them all: *This happened as it did for Hannah. You kept your promise as Hannah did and gave your baby back to the Lord. These wonderful new feelings of motherhood are for Melissa.*

I'd had many wonderful feelings of motherhood for Melissa, but I hadn't known these new ones even existed! You don't know what you're missing until you have it. Later, we did some calculations: it took three months to adopt Melissa, and this pregnancy was six months. The total was nine months. Often throughout the pregnancy I had prayed that Melissa would not feel left out with this new baby, and now this was part of the answer.

My last question had been, *What do I do now?* I had found myself complete as a woman, pregnant at last after so many years of longing and yearning for my womb to be filled. Now it would be empty again. God's answer gave me fresh hope: *Read the rest of Hannah's story.* I couldn't wait till morning to read my Bible. I turned to 1 Samuel:

> But Samuel was ministering before the Lord—a boy
> wearing a linen ephod. Each year his mother made him
> a little robe and took it to him when she went up with

her husband to offer the annual sacrifice. Eli would bless Elkanah and his wife, saying, "May the Lord give you children by this woman to take the place of the one she prayed for and gave to the Lord." Then they would go home. And the Lord was gracious to Hannah; she conceived and gave birth to three sons and two daughters. Meanwhile, the boy Samuel grew up in the presence of the Lord. (1 Samuel 2:18–21)

Wow! What He had done for Hannah, He intended to do for us! I was so filled with excitement; I could hardly wait for Ruben to come that morning! When Ruben finally came, his face reflected the same turmoil I'd felt when I first woke up expecting to be depressed. However, as soon as I shared what the Lord had done for me, he too received the joy and peace of knowing God was really still in charge and would make all things beautiful in His time.

The doctor had prescribed some antidepressants for me, but I didn't need them. God was my antidepressant! His promise and His strength helped me through. The hospital staff was very considerate of me, apologizing for the newborns crying across from my room. But even that did not take away the joy and peace that God had gifted me with. He knew the "whys" of everything. The verse my sister Anne later gave me was: *"And underneath are the everlasting arms"* (Deuteronomy 33:27). She said that we always know this, but when we're "down," we can actually *feel* them.

She came to visit the following day, fully expecting me to be very depressed. But she, too, experienced tremendous relief to find me at peace. She also shared something very special, which showed how much her heart had gone out to me the night of my labour and loss. Her in-laws had been over the evening that my baby was born. They had a prayer time for us around 10:30 that night. I believe that Jesus coming to me in the night with His comfort and peace was a direct answer to their prayers. In fact, one other thought I had when I had this "visitation" from the Lord was, *How can this be? I haven't spent hours in prayer seeking Him, but He has come anyway!* I felt weak spiritually, but the body of believers was strong on my behalf!

Many others prayed for us at this time, and this helped to build up our faith. We were not defeated; God had not blown a miracle. His ways are just and He does all things well. We received strength to carry on, always remembering what He had assured me of that night in the hospital room. Often I would feel my tummy and the reality of what had happened would hit me full-force. But the memory of His presence and words of promise always sustained me.

Several women came over and shared with me a miscarriage or stillbirth experience they'd had. This was a source of comfort and love which bonded us as women and members of Christ's body. God made sure I was loved, and used these times to bring healing to my heart. He always knew exactly what we needed. He was so gentle with us and often I felt He was carrying me as His little lamb.

Melissa was affected by this loss as well. She had eagerly shared with her friends that she would be having a baby brother or sister. However, her friends scoffed her, believing she was fabricating stories. Now when she needed her friends to stand by her, they seemed to be rejecting her.

We often prayed with her, explaining how the baby couldn't live because it hadn't lasted long enough inside Mommy's tummy to grow big enough. We also explained that we believed God would send another baby, but it would be in His time and in His way. She earnestly prayed for this every night. Her faith was so sweet and a real encouragement to us.

The new feelings of motherhood really *were* transferable! I felt a whole extra measure of protectiveness for Melissa that I hadn't had before, along with so much more grace and love. I wondered why I'd never known about this before, but now realized these instincts are a natural outcome of giving birth and every "natural" parent simply takes them for granted. I felt as if I'd been a "handicapped" parent and had not been able to overcome my handicap. Poor Melissa, I had failed her in many ways, but my heart was so full now—I loved my daughter in a new way. I loved my home and my husband like never before, and most of all I loved my God, the Giver and Sustainer of life. Because my daughter and husband were *mine*, I wanted to give them my best—my best caring, cooking, sewing, and loving. My creative abilities were now only there as tools with which to implement my love for my family.

These things may be so natural to others, and therefore it may seem strange to see them written down. For me, however, what I was now experiencing seemed to change my whole personality and outlook. I remember the day when I saw my kitchen in this new way—truly a tool to love my family. I went around in awe, and felt like hugging the cupboards, my new stove, fridge, and even my lovely dishes. I turned to look at my family, watching a Walt Disney movie at the dining room table. A beautiful new love for them dawned into my heart.

Ruben noticed my tears and came quietly to hold me, realizing that whatever was happening, it was an important moment to me. Since it was just a week since our baby had been born, he assumed this was the reason for my tears. Melissa saw the hugging session and tearfully came to join in. As I hugged her, I had such a longing for more children. It was almost unbearable, but it was a beautiful time of vulnerability and love; Jesus was binding us together, because we truly belonged together!

We felt a trip to Disneyworld would be a good idea at this time. We booked the trip and kept it a secret from Melissa until we celebrated an early Christmas. She was overjoyed when she opened the Disneyworld brochure! We had a wonderful time away and God blessed us with a special bonding time... just having fun together.

Psalm 63:3 says, *"Because thy loving kindness is better than life, my lips shall praise thee"* (KJV). A song based on these words kept coming to mind, and I kept singing it because it rang so true for me. Even though the life of my baby was very precious, His loving kindness, demonstrated through His gracious visit to me, was even more precious. It showed me that His strength was available to me in my deepest need and that His love weaves the colours of our earthly experiences into something different than we expect, but something more beautiful than we can imagine. His loving kindness was so real and taught me so much. I knew that this experience was invaluable. Some things cannot be learned in books; they have to be learned by experience.

CHAPTER TWELVE

Remember Not the Former Things

I saiah 43:18–19 says, *"Remember ye not the former things; neither consider the things of old. Behold, I will do a new thing; now it shall spring forth; shall ye not know it? I will even make a way in the wilderness, and rivers in the desert"* (KJV). Sometimes the loss of our baby seemed to be overwhelming, but the Lord gave this scripture to Ruben during one of these times.

Had I known for certain that we would have another one, I could have borne the loss. However, doubts of what had happened at the conference would engulf me. Were we really able to have children now, or was that just a "fluke" pregnancy... the only kind we'd ever have? I tried to keep busy and not leave time for brooding over these periodic doubts.

I was able to go back to my job as secretary, which was the best therapy I could have had. Also, the Lord gave me an enthusiasm for sewing; I had always enjoyed designing and sewing for Melissa and myself. As I clung to His promises and received His strength, I was gradually getting back my energy and enthusiasm for day-to-day life.

These scriptures also showed us how He still uses His words of long ago to inspire hope in His children today. We were to forget the past and not be remorseful of things that had been. God was at work in our present and future.

> I will pour out my Spirit on your offspring, and my bless-
> ing on your descendants. They will spring up like grass in
> a meadow, like poplar trees by flowing streams. One will
> say, "I belong to the Lord"; another will call himself by the
> name of Jacob; still another will write on his hand, "The
> Lord's," and will take the name Israel. (Isaiah 44:3–5)

Not only did the Lord confirm His promise of more children to us in this passage, He also prophesied them being anointed by Him. One of them calling himself by the name of Jacob was significant, because Ruben's second name was Jacob. We were encouraged to believe that Ruben would have more offspring! The prophecy at the conference had been to that effect as well. Our children would be anointed of the Lord! We had asked the Lord for a portion of scripture, and He had given us words from Ephesians 3:20—*"immeasurably more than all we ask or imagine."*

I knew I didn't want the past to become a remorseful cloud over the present. This would have resulted in more clouds of regret. The only way I could live in the present was to abide in Jesus, learn what He was trying to teach me, and be optimistic. Thus, during the next while, we had to lean on the Lord and His promise of more children. It wasn't easy, but we were so encouraged by the faith of our little Melissa, now eight years old, who continued to pray in faith that God would send us another baby in His time and in His way. The Lord gave us this in a scripture as well: *"But as for me, my prayer is unto thee, O Lord, in an acceptable time: O God, in the multitude of thy mercy hear me"* (Psalm 69:13. KJV) ...in His time and in His way.

The very thought that someone could experience the treasured blessing of children and not really want it, or take it for granted, was almost unbearable to me. We might want to trade blessings, but God is not a trading post. Even while God took our baby, He allowed many other unwanted babies to be born. He must have a plan in all this. It must be a beautiful plan, otherwise He would not have allowed such a deep disappointment in our lives.

Part of the reason was already plain to me. Even if I should never have another natural child, I knew that this one experience of childbirth would give me something precious to impact the rest of my life: I had discovered motherhood in its natural form. The Bible talks about a woman being saved in childbearing... perhaps that was a reference to what I was experiencing right now—a sense of ultimate fulfillment as a woman. I never used to understand all the mothers around me who were so content just to be at home, raising their families and living totally for them. In a way, I thought they seemed unenlightened, whereas I felt liberated and almost superior to them. But what I thought didn't affect any of them in the least. Deep down, I knew that I was the one who was "unliberated." I was missing this contentment, and it was a source of frustration and guilt.

As natural parents, we take for granted (and rightly so), the inherent knowledge upon giving birth that our babies are *ours.* With natural pregnancy comes the "instruction book," if you will, on how to bond with and take care of our babies. When you adopt, even though the papers legally tell you that this is now your baby, your heart doesn't necessarily know it. Given enough bonding, all this will come in time. After my childbirth experience, I knew firsthand what it was all about. I had received some of the maternal instincts that for me, at least, had come only through childbirth. This was truly the miracle I needed.

Hebrews 10:32–36 says:

> But recall the former days when, after you were enlightened, you endured a hard struggle with sufferings, sometimes being publicly exposed to reproach and affliction, and sometimes being partners with those so treated. For you had compassion on those in prison, and you joyfully accepted the plundering of your property, since you knew that you yourselves had a better possession and an abiding one. Therefore do not throw away your confidence, which has a great reward. For you have need of endurance, so that you have done the will of God you may receive what is promised. (ESV)

I found myself looking back with longing: where did my peaceful trusting go? Where was my extra close feeling for my husband? I felt it had been replaced with selfishness instead of patient waiting for the promise of the Lord to be fulfilled. This scripture was an answer to that prayer. The Hebrews referred to in this scripture had also undergone sufferings with joy—their possessions were plundered. But they were at peace, realizing they had better possessions in Christ. Apparently, they too forgot their struggles and lost their joyful zeal, just as I did. The author of Hebrews tells them not to throw away this confidence, but to always abide in the possessions we have in Christ.

Before I felt the Lord telling me not to remember what was past, not to dwell in remorse at the loss of our baby, but instead look forward to God giving us more children in the future. Now, however, when I found myself without a real spiritual hunger for God, I did not function with zeal as I once did. I was now to remember that zeal and get it back. How? By recalling the former days of strength and asking God's forgiveness in letting it slip, and then meditating on His Word. God fills in the "feelings" when we start with obedience.

CHAPTER THIRTEEN

New Beginnings

The following December, I knew something was happening. This was confirmed by the doctor early in January 1978—I was finally pregnant again. When we told Melissa, she asked, "Already?" Wow... the faith of a little child! We had thought it was taking a long time! Although we were again filled with great excitement, I soon experienced spotting, and with it came a sense of dread. *Not again... I don't want to lose this baby, too.*

No consoling of the doctor could turn my feelings into hope. Both Ruben and I did some soul-searching and, with the prayer of our friends Judith and Graham, we felt His peace about this baby. The fear left and shortly after that I experienced the baby's first movements. What a blessing that was, as if the baby herself was saying, "Don't worry, mommy, I'm still here..."

And "here" she stayed. Melissa was praying, "Please, Lord, let the baby last," referring to the previous baby not lasting long enough to be born alive. Well, the baby "lasted and lasted" until she was two weeks overdue and I was very big. My sister in Winnipeg had all three of her girls by Caesarean and I wondered if I'd have to go that route as well. But my doctor seemed quite confident that a natural birth would work in my case. Ruben and I had been to childbirth classes and were eagerly awaiting signs of labour. I was experiencing a lot of Braxton-Hicks contractions and asked my neighbour, who'd had ten children, about this. She assured me this was natural and not to worry.

Finally, the real contractions started. We had company at the time, so I tried to excuse myself. Eventually our guest left and we went to bed, knowing it was way too soon to go to the hospital. However, at two o'clock in the morning we did go in to the hospital, leaving a note for Melissa, who was ten by now.

As it turned out, it was still too soon. The contractions slowed down during the night and into the next day. I was told to do some walking. I was reminded that I was an "older mom," so things could take a while. Finally, around six o'clock that evening, the contractions started up again in earnest. Friends came by around that time and "encouraged" me by saying, "Hmmmm, that was a good one!" I silently disagreed; I had thought it was a rather bad one!

All through the night, with Ruben beside me and praying with me, we went through serious labour. I started to feel like pushing around 3:00 a.m. and was wheeled into the delivery room. Nothing happened, however, even after two hours of pushing. The easygoing doctor was finally worried and called an associate. They explained to me that they would do a forceps delivery, since the baby just wasn't coming out.

And it worked! I knew she was coming, because Ruben was starting to sniffle. And out she came, yelling lustily at the top of her lungs! (This must have launched her amazing singing voice!) She was placed on my belly and I saw a beautiful, robust, healthy baby girl. I wanted to cuddle her, but she was put into the isolette where Ruben spoke to her, gently welcoming her into our lives. She was absolutely focused on his face and words. It was truly a bonding moment. Even the doctors and nurses were sniffling as we praised God in that hushed little room! I weep even now as I write this. God in His amazing way brought us a miracle!

We named her Maria Rochelle, Maria after me and my mother. When the nurse brought her to me a while later, she said, "You have such a beautiful baby," to which I replied, "Yes, when God does a miracle, He goes all out!" I noticed also that Maria had her daddy's black hair and long, curly eyelashes! Wow... after all this time, all I had wanted was a baby, but God had given me the desire of my heart: a miniature Ruben!

Melissa was so happy as well... now she really did have a little sister! I stayed in the hospital for ten days due to complications; I had lost a lot of blood and fainted on my first attempt to get up. Even then, my doctor only let me go home because my nurse friend from British Columbia was staying with us. But at last, Maria and Mommy came home.

My friend had made delicious pork chops. She was so good at making me feel relaxed. She was also really good with Melissa, because she had two daughters who were the same age. We enjoyed her stay and appreciated the sacrifice she made. She had always told us there would be a "miniature Ruben" someday!

And so the blessing of natural parenthood finally became a reality for us. The bonding time we'd had with Melissa the past two years had been a Godsend, to say the least. We felt so close, so good as a family. Everyone was rejoicing with us and recognizing this as a true miracle of God.

When Maria was about six months old, we were back at the Holy Spirit conference in Brandon, this time for "show and tell." Everyone there praised God for Maria, the living proof of the miracle God had done for us!

I was nursing Maria and she was a healthy baby. Even the doctor was impressed: "Whatever you're doing, keep doing it," he said.

We loved watching Maria's little antics. When she got older, we gave her orange slices and she'd screw up her little face and shudder at the sourness. As we laughed at her, she'd smile and laugh, knowing she was our great entertainment!

CHAPTER FOURTEEN

Another New Beginning

Maria's arrival made us yearn for another child, so we prayed that God would send us a baby boy this time. I got pregnant right after that "prayer/homework" time! All along, I knew he'd be a boy. I had quit my secretarial job when I was seven months pregnant with Maria, so I was home now when all the pregnancy nausea came upon me.

At this time, I attended a weekly Bible study with some of my friends from the community. We met at each other's homes, and we always had a babysitter to look after the children. Although the pregnancy seemed to progress well, I felt there would again be a lesson to be learned. I actually pleaded with God to let me learn it "from a book," instead of another "experience." I shared this with our Bible study group. Again, the Lord gave me His peace.

The due date was in mid-June and the doctors decided not to let this one be overdue. On June 13, 1980, I was in the hospital getting prepped for the next day when they were going to induce labour. There were two empty beds, one with a pink bedspread and the other with a blue one. I could choose, the nurse said. I chose the blue one, saying, "It's going to be a boy!"

The next morning, June 14, they took me to the labour room and put me on the drip. I didn't feel any pain and the doctor didn't think I was doing much. However, I was, and around three o'clock the doctor was quickly summoned because I wanted to push. When he finally came, the cord was wrapped around the baby's head twice and I was told to stop pushing. I had no idea what was happening and found out how hard it is to stop pushing once you've started! Finally, our baby boy came and was also placed on my belly. It was the day before Father's Day, and I said to Ruben, "Happy Father's Day!" We were rejoicing... God had blessed us with a big baby boy! He was nine pounds, five ounces.

We named him Nathaniel Reuben, the second name after his father. Later on, we realized the significance of the names we had chosen: Nathaniel meant "asked of God" and Reuben meant "behold, a son." This reflected our experience exactly!

However, I noticed that he seemed "floppy" and somewhat distressed. The doctor didn't say much at the time, but I found out later that he also had his suspicions and was keeping a close eye on Nathan right from his birth.

It was Ruben's sister's twenty-fifth anniversary the next day, and I told the doctor I felt well enough to go! Even though the doctor gave me permission, the nurse, a friend of mine, came to me and discouraged me from doing so. Ruben took the girls and went to Steinbach for this event, thinking all was well with me and Nathan. They came back late and made a quick stop at the hospital around 10:30 that evening. Maria was so excited. Her voice rang out throughout the hospital: "I'm going to see the baby, oh yes, mmm hummm" ("Oh yes, mmm hummm" was her favourite saying). And see him she did! However, baby Nathan didn't seem happy and she became sad, saying, "The baby is tying"—of course, she meant "crying." We tried to reassure her, but we were worried as well.

The next day, the doctor finally came and talked to us. He wanted to do a spinal tap on Nathan because he suspected bleeding in the head, perhaps due to birth trauma. We gave our permission and waited, dreading the results. I refused all visitors at this point; even my pastor's wife was turned away. When the doctor came back with our crying baby, the news was grim: yes, there was evidence of blood in the spinal fluid. This was not good, so we were sent off to Winnipeg, to the Children's Hospital where I had worked years before.

We took a friend along to sit with Maria in the back seat while we drove to Winnipeg by car; an ambulance was not recommended, as the ride was too bumpy. This added to our fear and we drove as carefully as we could. Once in Winnipeg, we took our friend to the bus depot where she headed back to Neepawa. Maria would stay with us until my sister came to take care of her. Melissa stayed in Neepawa with a friend of ours so she wouldn't miss school.

Nathan was placed in an isolette in the Intensive Care Nursery. Preemies were usually the ones occupying the isolettes, so it seemed much too small for our big baby boy. Tests were done, but the results took a while, so Nathan was in there for a few days. We spent a lot of time with Nathan and I continued to try nursing him. Nursing had been difficult from the beginning; the effort seemed too much for him and he preferred the easy-flowing bottle. But the doctor's challenge was for him to easily achieve this, and after a few days Nathan passed the test. Tests showed that there had been a small mass above his optic nerve, but he was allowed to go home... the bleeding in his head had dissipated.

He still seemed to have a bit of a fever, so we were uneasy about taking him home. He was discharged on a Sunday and we went to our former church, where Ron and Anne were directing a children's musical. Afterwards the pastor and some of the deacons came into the nursery to pray for Nathan. We were much encouraged and took him home; the fever was gone!

But we were not out of the woods yet and we were to come back for more appointments. I noticed that when I tried to get Nathan to follow a toy, he seemed to be able to do it but would eventually roll his eyes back too far. I became concerned about blindness or some other eye problem. I even took him to our local doctor to get checked. The doctor examined him, but didn't come up with anything conclusive. Our happy time with our first son was clouded with uncertainty. We had to trust that our God was working behind the clouds and would make things clear in His time.

When it was time for his next appointment in Winnipeg, we wanted his eyes especially to be checked. After the doctor finished his examination, he waited quietly until I got Nathan dressed.

"Well, Nathan isn't blind," he said. "But there is something much more seriously wrong. Nathan will be hydrocephalic."

We knew immediately what this was: *water on the brain*. It seemed that when the blood had settled in his head, it had blocked the drainage for his cranial fluid. This caused his head to swell, which of course we had not noticed. The doctor went on to explain that he could have a tube inserted through surgery and the fluid would drain off. This tube was called a shunt; it would need replacing from time to time, and we'd have to keep a close eye on Nathan for headaches indicating a blocked tube. In any case, it was not life-threatening.

This was bittersweet news to us; all we knew was that our troubles were not over yet. Now Nathan would need surgery! It was slated for the end of August, when he would be seven weeks old.

Nathan was such a sweet little baby, never demanding and always relaxed and happy. He didn't seem to be in any pain; he was bright and a real joy to all of us. We couldn't bear the thought of him having to be in the hospital again, so when a friend said they were going to have a prayer meeting especially for him she asked me what they should pray for. "Pray that he won't need the surgery," I said.

As the surgery date neared, we knew we'd have to take him in. They gave me the shaver to shave off his nice, dark hair. That was hard, but I made sure to keep a lock for his baby book. Then he was wheeled into surgery. We had asked earlier if they would check the size of his head to see if it had gotten smaller, but they brushed this idea aside and it was never done.

We left the hospital during the surgery because it was all so traumatic. But afterward, we came right back. We arrived at Nathan's room, but he wasn't there. However, there was a card from our former Winnipeg pastor and on it was the famous poem "Footprints in the Sand." I had never seen it before and was rather moved and puzzled at the same time. What did this mean and why hadn't we stayed? The surgeon had tried to contact us right after the surgery, but he had now left the hospital.

We went to see Nathan, who was still in ICU. He seemed all right, although the nurse said he had low blood pressure. She urged us to call the doctor, which we did. Ruben had written out some questions to ask and, as he was talking to the surgeon, I could see him writing down the answers in very shaky handwriting.

I knew it was scary. He told me that the surgeon was concerned because he normally drained the excess fluid first and then inserted the tube. However, he hadn't found any fluid and suspected that it had already absorbed into Nathan's brain. He could end up being a vegetable. He had inserted the tube anyway. This was a very negative prognosis, indeed, and I found myself fainting. Ruben and the nurse caught me and we were led to the parents' room, where we could recover from our emotional upheaval. Immediately I remembered the Footprints poem and said, "Lord, carry us now."

After a while, we prayed together and then wanted nothing more than to go back to Nathan. We had decided that he was our boy and we would love him to wholeness, no matter what. Nathan seemed the same to us, except that he was experiencing nausea from the anaesthesia. After he threw up, he settled down and fell asleep. When we felt he was okay, we went back to my brother's place.

On our way to the hospital the next day, I had a sudden revelation: we had often prayed that God would allow the spinal fluid to drain naturally. Perhaps that was the reason the surgeon hadn't found any fluid: God Himself had drained it! He probably hadn't needed the surgery at all... just like I had asked my friend to pray! Two other people also said the same thing to us; they didn't believe the doctor's report and thought Nathan would be okay. Nathan quickly recovered from the surgery and soon we were able to take him home.

For some reason, we were never able to get a hold of the surgeon to ask more questions, but we found out at our appointment a few weeks later that he had nothing but negative expectations. He asked whether Nathan had experienced convulsions and a few other nasty things that sounded scary, but we said, "No, he seems to be doing very well." The doctor was pleasantly surprised and another appointment was set for a few months down the road to check him again. The development doctor said she didn't need to see him anymore and we knew from the way Nathan was behaving that he was perfectly okay.

The surgeon himself said this when we went back to him about a year after his surgery. He actually scratched his head and said the words we were waiting to hear: "I don't think he ever needed this surgery." We looked at each other and praised God. The sky was clear, the clouds were gone, and our Nathan was really okay! And he didn't need that shunt!

They were hesitant to remove it, however, and therefore it is there to this day. Sometimes it bothers him when he turns his head and he experiences headaches. But he really is okay!

We just enjoyed our two little ones and our teenaged Melissa. Maria was so delighted to have a little "bwuzzo"—brother. She was very possessive of him. One day, when they were a little older, I gave them each a treat and she wanted him to say the magic words. So he did, saying, "Peanut butter sandwiches." But in this case, she had wanted him to say, "Thank you." He was remembering what he'd learned on Sesame Street, where "peanut butter sandwiches" were the magic words.

I had been doing a little dialogue with Maria. I'd say, "Who's a sweet little girl?" She would reply, "Me." I did this from when she was very little. So now I included Nathan, too. I started by saying, "Who's a sweet little girl?" And Maria replied, "Me." Then I asked little Nathan, "Who's a sweet little boy?" And he also replied, "Me." Then, unrehearsed, Maria said, "Who's a sweet little mommy?" I was so overwhelmed. It was the most rewarding moment ever!

Another time, we were already living in our new, unfinished house on our acreage. Maria was playing house, using the construction scaffolding as her wash line. She would play being the mother. We were not allowed to hug or kiss her when she was wearing her white shoes... they identified her "mommy status." Nathan, of course, was her little charge and when he hurt himself and started to cry, she asked him if he wanted "Mommy" to kiss it better. But he continued to cry, so she asked if she should take him to his "stepmother"? Well, I never! I heard all this from the next room, where I was nursing our new baby.

Yes, we had one more! David Patrick graced us with his presence on January 3, 1984, when we didn't think we'd have anymore. We actually thought we were getting too old, so we were being careful. But then Ruben thought, *Oh well, maybe God has unhealed me,* and we threw "careful" out the window! In my heart, I knew we weren't finished having babies, so imagine our delight when we found out we were expecting again! It was further proof that God doesn't "unheal" people!

I had lost quite a bit of weight after Nathan, but now I was gaining a lot. The doctor thought this baby could be twelve pounds! He was due December 17, but the New Year came and went and he still hadn't arrived. We had bought the kids each a Care Bear, and his was a birthday bear. If only he'd come and have his "birth" day!

The doctors had me come into the hospital on January 2 to monitor me and check the baby for signs of stress. They decided to send me to Brandon for a C-section to avoid another difficult birth. Because I didn't feel any pain, I didn't think I was having contractions, although there were regular "tightenings" as we drove by ambulance to Brandon. During this trip, I shared my testimony with the nurse who came along. Near Minnedosa, the Neepawa doctor called and asked them to check me for dilation. But I refused, thinking that nothing was happening.

Boy, was I wrong! When we got to Brandon, the doctor there examined me and found me almost fully dilated! He wasn't going for the C-section idea... he would just break the water and the baby would come! We asked him to give us a moment to decide what to do. We had prayed that God would give the doctors guidance, so we realized that He was giving this doctor the best idea. We advised him to go ahead. After he broke the water, there was hard labour (which I could definitely feel) for about an hour, and then there was David Patrick!

Wow! Everything happened so fast; David was whisked away by the paediatrician for a quick check, pronounced okay, and then returned to my room at the hospital. I noticed that David tended to choke when I nursed him; the staff told me he had been born so fast that his mucous hadn't been expelled yet. They always kept an eye on this and suctioned him at times. After a while, he was fine. The next morning I had surgery to have my tubes tied; we thought maybe I was getting a little too old for more babies! I was thirty-eight.

But we sure enjoyed this one. What a fun-loving little guy David turned out to be. Both of our boys had my hair colour and all three kids had my brown eyes. Melissa had her dad's colour of eyes. They were such a sweet bunch.

By this time, Melissa was taking her high school at Steinbach Bible College, so she missed out on a lot. However, she came home just after David was born. She'd been home throughout the Christmas break, waiting for him. But he didn't come and she had to go back. Then, right in the middle of that first night back, her daddy called to tell her the news. She came home that weekend with her grandparents, scolding baby David for putting her through this unnecessary travel!

As mentioned, we now lived on an acreage just west of town. Ruben was building our dream home. He had friends helping him, but it would be awhile until it was finished. Ruben wondered if he should be working on the house, since he thought the loud hammering would disturb the baby. But I told him the baby had heard this right through the pregnancy and would miss the background noise. I would, too; I wanted the house finished!

In fact, David's first word was "hamma" (hammer). His favourite toy was his rubber "hamma," which we almost lost at a nephew's wedding. As parents, we know that favourite toys *cannot* be lost!

As Maria grew older and went to school, she was very concerned for her friends' salvation. Usually her prayers at night included, "Please let them all become Christians." One night she realistically included, "At least some of them."

Nathan was very neat in his schoolwork, sometimes at the expense of not getting his work finished. The kids often asked to be homeschooled, and we felt God wanted us to heed their request. And so we did, for about five and a half years. At that point, I got a full-time job in the Activity Department at our local nursing home. We had heard about a Christian school not too far away and felt we should send them there. David was in the middle of his fourth grade and became quite concerned that he wouldn't "be smart enough." After all, only his mother had taught him and it had been way too easy thus far. The real school would be much harder. I told him he would laugh at himself when he discovered how smart he really was.

Sure enough, when they returned after their first day, he was smiling. "Guess what, Mom?" he asked. "I got skipped into Grade Five!"

All three of them really enjoyed this school. Of course, I missed their cuteness, which I had so enjoyed when I homeschooled them. But I heard of their cuteness at school: the teacher was a newlywed and had showed the class her Valentine's Day card from her husband, complete with coupons for kisses. "Oh," David said. "My mom and dad don't need coupons for kissing!"

Another cute incident happened with Nathan when he was about three years old. The bleeding in his head as an infant might have been the cause for him being cross-eyed. We took all three of them to a children's eye specialist in Winnipeg. The doctor put drops in his eyes and told us to come back in half an hour. So we took them downstairs for a snack of crackers and juice. Nathan seemed quite perturbed and finally blurted out, "I can't eat these crackers; they're blurry!" Just before he entered Kindergarten, he had surgery on his eye and the cross-eyed condition was almost perfectly resolved thanks to this excellent surgeon.

Nathan was the linguist in our family, teaching David accuracy in pronunciation as he learned to talk. David didn't get away with words like "cwib"; he had to say "crib"!

Often when I tucked David in at night, he would ask for a Tiny Moose story. He told me he had an imaginary friend named Tiny Moose, so he and I would create amazing stories of his adventures with Tiny Moose, always with a practical or spiritual application. The only one I can still remember, though, is the one where Tiny Moose goes home and tells his mother another David story and his mother says, "Isn't it nice that our Tiny Moose has this imaginary friend named 'David'?"

CHAPTER FIFTEEN

Our Miracles Today

We always told people we believed in miracles, because we had three of them pattering around in our home every day. Each child is, of course, a miracle and Melissa, our adopted daughter, definitely is one, too—but our three natural-born children were not supposed to be here, according to medical science. We want to give God all the glory for our wonderful family.

Melissa went on a mission's trip after her Grade Eleven year at SBI. The mission started off with "Boot Camp," a very challenging experience for her. However, her letters were still full of humour and a delight to read. On the trip, she was involved in music ministry and building houses for the poor. When she came home, she knew what she wanted to do with her life: develop her musical talents for Christian service.

So, after her graduation from Steinbach Bible School, she entered Brandon University where she took three years of music. Twice she was also music minister at churches in Brandon; in between that, she was always helping with music at her own church, Bethel Christian Assembly. We went to this church for a time as well, for a time of healing and refreshing.

Difficult circumstances prompted Melissa to move to Airdrie, Alberta, where she met a young man whom she eventually married. They had their wedding here in Neepawa in the beautiful Presbyterian Church. After a while, they had three beautiful daughters—Taylor, Whitney, and Gabriella. Her husband got a very good job offer in Houston, Texas, so they left Alberta and moved to the sunny south. This is where the two younger girls were born. Just before their tenth anniversary, however, the marriage broke down completely, ending in divorce. Now, six years later, she is happily married to John Kerr, and they are settled in the outskirts of Houston, Texas.

Melissa has always been very musical, having won several awards during her teen years, especially in singing. People often commented that she could "sing like an angel," a talent she has passed on to her daughters, and Whitney especially seems to be headed for a singing career. Melissa teaches music in a preschool program in her church and has many piano students as well. She has also been involved in praise and worship in various churches. Our three granddaughters are a great delight to us, and although we don't see them nearly often enough, it's always wonderful when we are together.

Maria always wanted to be a teacher. She took ballet as a young girl but told us one day that she would no longer be able to do so, as she was going to be a teacher. (I guess she couldn't envision herself as both a ballerina and a teacher). She went to Providence College for a year, then finished her Bachelor of Education degree at Brandon University. She took piano lessons all along, writing her exams until she attained a Grade 10 standing in piano. She has been a music/science/health/math teacher in Carberry Elementary School for the last eight years and really enjoys her job. She lives in a condo in Brandon where she is very involved with music in her church. There's a special anointing on her when she leads worship. Her friends are also a major part of her life; she seems to be the life of the party!

Nathan also started off at Providence College, where he earned a degree in Intercultural Studies as well as a diploma in TESOL (Teaching English to Speakers of Other Languages). He was always interested in languages and took German as an extra subject in high school. We never taught our children the Low German language, and Nathan especially wished we would have. He learned some Korean and was once told by a Korean that he had no accent at all. He used his TESOL training after graduation by going to South Korea for a few months to teach English in an elementary school. He then finished his Education degree at the University of Winnipeg and now teaches at a Christian school in Winnipeg. In December 2010, he became engaged to a wonderful girl named Stephanie Kroeker. Because Stephanie speaks Low German quite well, he is learning it after all and having a lot of fun using it with us!

David was always the adventurous one: hunting, camping "survival style," and dirt-biking! He has a creative flair in all his activities. Both Nathan and David graduated from our local high school. When

David was to be given the Industrial Arts award, he didn't want to receive it because it would be considered favouritism—after all, his dad was the teacher. But when Ruben explained that he would not be the only recipient of the award, David was proud to accept it. He worked for a year after high school and then went on to the Master's Commission at Calvary Temple in Winnipeg. There he met Jodi Barker, a fun-loving girl who definitely caught his attention! They were married the following year and now live in Winnipeg. He went on to be in a four-year aircraft mechanics apprenticeship program, which he completed in the summer of 2010. He works at St. Andrew's Airport in Winnipeg as a licensed aircraft maintenance engineer. Jodi is a gifted photographer and is very busy. They are quite involved at Calvary Temple, where David is an amazing drummer.

There's so much more that a mother could share about her children. Ruben and I are so thankful for God's intervention in our lives—His gift of salvation, His gift of family, and His daily mercies and grace. We're also very thankful that all of our children are following the Lord.

In regards to my family, my dad retired to a nursing home in Warman and became a very peaceful and loving man in his later years. He died in 1990, just before his eighty-fifth birthday, leaving us with sweet memories and even a small monetary legacy which he had somehow managed to save from his meagre pension.

The rest of my siblings are all more or less retired, just like us! Four of us live in Manitoba, having met our spouses at Steinbach Bible College.

My brother Henry passed away just after his sixty-fifth birthday, having suffered for a long time with emphysema. We had all been with him the week before, celebrating with singing and presenting him with a memory album. When we sang "O Happy Day," he turned to me and said, "It is a happy day". How thankful we were to have all been there with him before he went on to be with the Lord.

Bill was a professor at Providence College for many years. He and Maryrose now live in an apartment near The Forks in Winnipeg. They have one son and one grandson, whom they enjoy very much.

John, the oldest brother, lives in B.C. with his wife Pat. He retired from a successful career of drafting homes. Two of his children live in Saskatoon and one lives in Calgary. He often asks us to move to "paradise" with him. Recently, that region suffered from many forest fires. Ruben pointed out that this so-called "paradise" seemed more like "purgatory" to him!

My brother Abe, along with his wife Mary and their oldest son and his family, live in B.C. as well. His other two sons live in Calgary and Saskatoon. Abe had a successful family-operated sign-painting business in Saskatoon for many years. They are now enjoying their two grandsons in B.C.

Dick and Helen were always involved in ministry (Dick was a pastor). They have now retired to Warman, where they are closer to their children and grandchildren.

My younger brother Ike was a sign painter and has retired as well. However, he has now taken it up again as a private business. (Retirement seems to be an elusive term for them, too!) He and his wife Bonnie live in Winnipeg. They have two married children and several grandchildren whom they really enjoy.

Anne, the youngest, married Ron Derksen, and they live in Winnipeg as well. Anne was a determined young student who practiced hard. We had no piano, so she went to our unheated church in Warman to practice. She eventually obtained her ARCT (Associate of the Royal Conservatory of Toronto) certificate in piano after their third daughter was born. We're very proud of her, and she's been teaching piano all these years. Their three daughters live in Winnipeg and are married with children.

I worked for many years as a nurse's aide, and then as the Adult Day Program Coordinator at our local nursing home. I also took many related courses along the way. When I retired in December 2003, we went to Houston to be with Melissa and her family for Christmas. The other children joined us there as well. From there, we went to Brownsville, Texas, to help in a mission that builds homes for the poor and operates a child sponsorship program in Mexico. Nathan was with us, too, having just finished his English teaching job in Korea. He was my inspiration.

When we came back home, I enrolled in the TESOL course offered at Steinbach Bible College, where I'd graduated in 1967 with a General Bible diploma. Going back to school was one of the hardest things I'd ever done. It wasn't easy to leave my home, but Ruben came to visit me regularly and in April 2004 I graduated again, this time with a Bachelor of Arts in TESOL... in my old age, yet!

I have been very busy teaching English and really enjoy meeting immigrants. Ruben helped me as well, for a while. He had retired from his teaching job at our local high school in 1999. He taught Industrial Arts there for twenty-five years.

We had a family-operated strawberry farm on our acreage, which started off as just a hobby. This turned into a more serious venture after he retired from teaching. Our summers were very busy with our children also quite involved in the strawberry farm. But now, after twenty years of operation, we have ploughed down all the strawberries. Ruben, however, will always be a farmer and is looking into growing something that is a lot less work.

We are trying to retire, recognizing that we have reached that age, and so we are looking forward to traveling, doing things together as a family and hopefully having more grandchildren! Ruben and I always anticipated retirement as an opportunity to do things together, and so far have enjoyed some travel and teaching ESL together. We also like sharing this story of what God's done in our lives, and have done so at several different meetings. Ours has been an amazing love story, for which we are very thankful.

Looking back on my life's journey, I realize that the hand of God has been guiding me all the way. My mother's intuitive sense of my destiny, and her cooperation with what she sensed God wanted to do in my life, were very precious to me. Someone once said that the reason we are here is to show a facet of God that only our individual uniqueness can portray. God uses each of us uniquely according to the gifts He has given us. I am honoured to have been chosen to mother the children we have. We firmly believe that were it not for the miraculous intervention of God, they would not be here!

I trust you have been blessed by our story and encouraged in your heart to expect great things from Him as well. He looks to the heart, loves us more deeply than we can ever know, and wants us to trust

Him just like we want our children to trust us, to believe that we only want the best for them.

I pray a blessing on you, my readers, and welcome your own comments or stories. Maybe you, too, are "another Hannah," or "another Abraham," or someone else in the Bible who you can relate to.

We all have a story about the goodness of God in our lives, a story that needs to be shared and celebrated—just like this one!

Epilogue

A lot has happened in our family since the writing of *Another Hannah* in June of 2011. Ruben and I have prayed a lot about what to do with our former strawberry fields. We finally had peace about subdividing it, which is now in progress. New things are happening in the lives of our children as well, and here is what they have to say:

One of the things I will always remember as a kid was knowing that no matter what, my parents loved each other. I took great security in that fact (even if I didn't realize it then) and I believe it has shaped how I view my own marriage today. I look to my parents and their faith in God and how through the seasons of their life, when they were unsure of what lay ahead, they trusted in God. My lovely wife Jodi and I are in the midst of growing our own family and we are excited for what the future holds for us. God has richly blessed us and we so appreciate the role our parents have played in our lives and how they continue to be an integral part of our new young family.

—David, Jodi and Gemma

We were married August 6, 2011, shortly after *Another Hannah* was published. Our passion is to serve Him as a witness...in all our activities and relationships we want to "spread the love". God has expanded that passion to spread His love by surprising us with a double blessing of twins to arrive early in the New Year. We pray each and every day for these beautiful babies and are making the choice to surrender their future and our journey through parenting to our Wonderful Counselor. Ephesians 3:20 says, "Now all glory to God, who is able through His mighty power at work within us, to accomplish infinitely more than we might ask or think" (NLT).

—Nathaniel and Stephanie

Since the publishing of *Another Hannah*, I have continued to work in Carberry, Manitoba, teaching K-4 music half time and grade 4 math/science/health half time. My days are very fulfilling as I impart to children the joys of learning. I am still leading worship in my church in Brandon, and am also involved in two different choirs. God has blessed me with many things in life but above all I am the most thankful for my family. The closeness we share, the many different ways he opens doors for us and brings us through life's milestones - these are all evidence to me that God is still working miracles in our family on a daily basis. Nowadays, not all of the miracles are larger-than-life as are the ones you have just read in my mom's book, but all of them are evidence of a loving God with an amazing plan for us.

—Maria

We are so very proud of mom's accomplishment in writing *Another Hannah*. It is a story that has blessed many readers, including us! Sometimes the pages of life flip so fast that details are forgotten, so it was special to be reminded of how our story unfolded over the years. What stands out most for me is God's faithfulness...constantly loving, comforting and leading. In spite of disappointments, it is now clear to me how God's plan was unfolding, one section at a time. Thank you, Mom & Dad, for letting Him be your guide and believing that He was still in the Miracle Business! That proves to me now, in a time of transition for my family, He can and will do it again.

—Melissa

Mari: I will close with more from Melissa: "Thank you, mom, for reminding us of the importance of writing down our story. Not just for us, but so that others will see and know how great our God is!! We promise to keep it going and remind our children that when things don't make sense, hold on like never before to the promise in His word... "to give you a hope and a future...to prosper you" (Jeremiah 29:11)...holding on, just like Grandma and Grandpa did!"

Photo Album

Anne, Mari and Ike
(the "Derksen trio")

Mari (right) with cousin Mary,
off to Bible School

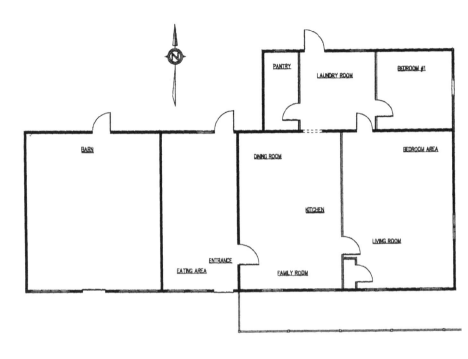

The floorplan of the home as illustrated
by John Derksen

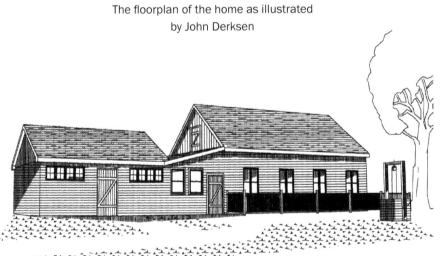

A sketch of Mari's childhood home in Reinland
as illustrated by John Derksen

CLOCKWISE, STARTING TOP LEFT
1. Mari in 1965
2. Ruben and Mari's wedding day
3. Now we're a family with Melissa
4. Mari, pregnant at last!

TOP LEFT: All our
miracles together

TOP RIGHT: Here they are,
all grown up

LEFT: Ruben and Mari's
25th Wedding Anniversary

Family Photo

Ruben and Mari's
40th Wedding Anniversary

The Klassen family in the
summer of 2010

TOP LEFT: Melissa as a baby
TOP RIGHT: Melissa's Grade Twelve graduation
CENTRE: Melissa with her three daughters

Melissa and her husband, John

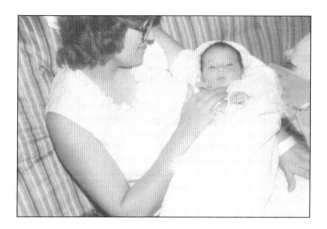

TOP: Maria as a baby
LEFT: Maria as a child
RIGHT: Maria's university graduation

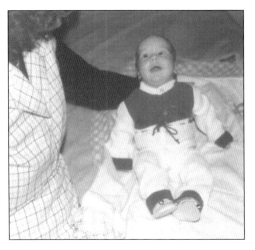

TOP: Nathan as a baby
RIGHT: Nathan as a child
LEFT: Nathan's college graduation

Nathan with his fiancée, Stephanie

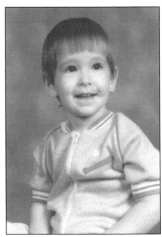

CLOCKWISE, STARTING TOP LEFT
1. David as a baby
2. David as a child
3. David's Grade Twelve graduation
4. David and Jodi on their rainy wedding day

The Angel of the Lord

Words and music by Mari Klassen, July, 1976
Arr. by Maria Klassen, Feb/11

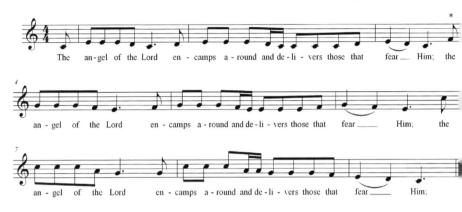

* When 1st singer finishes, 2nd singer begins here...also 3rd.

"The angel of the LORD encamps around those who fear him, and he delivers them" (Psalm 34:7, NIV).

The author welcomes your questions and feedback regarding *Another Hannah*. Mari may be contacted via email: mari.klassen@hotmail.com

Mari with her siblings. Left to right, Issac, John, Helena, Abe, Henry (sitting), Mari, Bill and Anne

From left to right: Nathan and Stephanie (pregnant with twins), Maria, Ruben and Mari, David with Gemma and wife Jodi (also pregnant), Melissa (under Gemma) and her three girls in front; left to right: Whitney, Taylor and Gabriella. Taken summer of 2013 at Lester Beach, Man. at our family holiday.
photo by: www.photosbyjodi.com